The Handbook of Strange But True Facts

Compiled by
Clifford Sawhney

PUSTAK MAHAL®

Publishers
Pustak Mahal®

Administrative office and sale centre
J-3/16 , Daryaganj, New Delhi-110002
☎ 23276539, 23272783, 23272784 • *Fax:* 011-23260518
E-mail: info@pustakmahal.com • *Website:* www.pustakmahal.com

Branches
Bengaluru: ☎ 080-22234025 • *Telefax:* 080-22240209
E-mail: pustak@airtelmail.in • pustak@sancharnet.in
Mumbai: ☎ 022-22010941, 022-22053387
E-mail: rapidex@bom5.vsnl.net.in
Patna: ☎ 0612-3294193 • *Telefax:* 0612-2302719
E-mail: rapidexptn@rediffmail.com

ISBN 978-81-223-0839-2

Edition: 2013

Printed at : **Sharma Printers, Delhi**

Dedication

This book is dedicated to my maternal aunt, Ms Edna Coelho.

Without her selfless assistance and guidance, half the battles of life would never have been won.

Acknowledgement

The strange but true facts in this book have been garnered from multiple sources, which include the print media, electronic media, books, websites and oral accounts. Likewise, the pictures have come from numerous sources. Sincere thanks to one and all of these sources, since it is not possible to individually acknowledge each and every source. Thanks also to Mr Ram Avtar Gupta, MD, Pustak Mahal, for agreeing to publish this book and to Mr S.K. Roy and other staffer members for their support.

Preface

Strange but true facts hold a fascination for every individual and the author is no exception. Occasionally, strange facts hit one square on the jaw and set the mind thinking. For instance, why would the Puffer fish be a delicacy in Japan when its poison is 500 times deadlier than cyanide and there is no known antidote?

At other times, the strange facts happen to be sitting right under our noses and we never take notice. In this category are two words, *lakh* and *crore*, which are not English words at all, although English-speaking Indians have been using them for generations as legal English tender!

The facts in this book span every gamut of human and non-human affairs and would be of interest to readers with widely differing palates.

This first edition of *The Handbook of Strange But True Facts* is simply the beginning. There are literally hundreds and thousands of strange but true facts that could not be incorporated in the first edition due to space constraints. As the years and the editions advance, a game of musical chairs will ensure that "old" facts fall by the wayside to allow a berth for "new" facts.

Readers are welcome to write in with their comments or to submit new facts at: cliffsaw@rediffmail.com.

—Clifford Sawhney

Contents

SECTION-I

India

SECTION-II

The World

Section I

India

Animal Affairs

The Strange Love Affair of a Leopard and Cow

You have heard of inter-caste marriages, but have you heard of an inter-species affair between two animals that are traditional enemies? This real-life incident has unfolded at Antoli village, Vadodara District, Gujarat. The couple in the limelight are a year-old leopard and a three-year-old cow!

Since early October 2002, the sleeping habits of villagers from Antoli have changed, after the discovery of the late evening rendezvous between the strange "couple". Sometime around midnight, the sinewy form of the leopard emerges from the maize fields and stealthily enters the village. After a careful *dekko* of the surroundings, the feline pads his way silently towards a clearing where a cow has been tethered. A few yards away, some goats are also tied.

Having inched its way to the cow, the leopard slowly rolls over on its back, raises its paw in the air and puts it gently on the cow's head, all the while making purring sounds. The cow reciprocates, lets out a soft "moo" and licks the leopard. After quite some time of this "necking", the leopard sits up, as the cow licks it intermittently.

All the while, the villagers look on from the shadows, barely 20 metres away, overawed and speaking in hushed tones in an atmosphere that is charged with electric tension. Not very pleased with the close human proximity, much before daybreak, the leopard decides to call it a day.

Reveals Rohit Vyas, honorary wildlife warden of Vadodara: "We have been keeping a watch, but unfortunately the frequency of the leopard's visits have reduced. It's really surprising the way these animals behave."

Comments conservator of forests, Vadodara, HS Singh: "Sometimes animal behaviour can get modified. In this case, it is probably because the leopard has passed the sub-adult stage, lives in a rural area and is not strictly in a wild environment."

Perhaps if the traditional animal enemies in Gujarat could take to "kissing" each other, we humans - in Gujarat and elsewhere - could learn a thing or two about togetherness from them.

Dogs Lack Some Senses

Dogs may have a sharp sense of hearing, but are lacking in some other senses. For instance, did you know that dogs cannot see as well as humans? And like many other animals, they are considered colour blind.

A dog first detects an object by its movement, second by its brightness and third by its shape. Of course, it also uses its sense of smell to recognise the object, when close up.

Animal Matchmaking Through Website

Matchmaking is a tough calling. More so if you are into matchmaking for animals! And the Central Zoo Authority (CZA) should know just how tough it is. Concerned about the growing band of eligible bachelors in Indian zoos, the CZA recently launched a website where lonely captive animals will find their soul mates.

According to CZA member-secretary PR Sinha, many zoos have only male or female animals of some species and are hard pressed to find suitable partners for their lonely wards. The launch of the website, www.cza.nic.in, is meant to solve that problem. There are 165 CZA-recognised zoos in India, of which 58 are major ones and the others happen to be mini zoos or deer parks.

With the launch of the website, zoo authorities have to simply log onto www.cza.nic.in and find the right match for their ward. Thereafter, they simply approach the concerned zoo and have their problem sorted out. Unlike humans, in most cases, says Sinha, the male will be sent to the female's zoo.

The website has already achieved some measure of success, with the Hyderabad zoo receiving a female rhino from the Kanpur zoo for its lonely male rhino. And the Kanpur zoo, which has two female foxes, will be receiving three male and three female foxes. Likewise, the Sepahijala zoo near Agartala is receiving a female rhino from the Agartala zoo.

Incredibly, dowry is beginning to play spoilsport, just as it does in human affairs! Some zoo officials don't realise the importance of having a wide variety of animals. They refuse to part with an animal if they have only one of a species. They are only willing to relent after some tough bargaining about what they will receive in return for the creature they have in their custody. This only ensures that the animal and the species in question suffer.

A classic case in point is that of the cheetah. The last Indian cheetahs were shot dead in 1948. After Independence, India imported 49 hunting cheetahs, with several zoos even taking a solitary cheetah, when having a pair made more sense to ensure the continuity of the species. Fifty years down the line, not a single hunting cheetah survives from the 49 imported ones.

This time around, perhaps, better sense will prevail.

Animal Sacrifice Still Prevalent in Orissa

India may supposedly be a country where *ahimsa* prevails and the cow is worshipped, but lakhs of goats, sheep, buffaloes and cocks were sacrificed during pujas across the country, particularly Orissa, in 2002. This, despite protests from animal rights activists and laws that specifically prohibit the sacrifice of animals for religious purposes.

The majority of people in Orissa still sacrifice animals to gratify their mother goddess, although some have taken to the compassionate practice of sacrificing cucumbers and gourds. Although the practice of animal sacrifice is prevalent in villages, people in cities and towns also indulge in the heinous tradition.

Explains sociologist Rita Ray: "In Devi worship, power is concentrated in the blood. Blood has been the symbol of reproduction and regeneration. Hence, animal sacrifice has been practised by Shakti cult believers."

Ray reveals that Devi worship is prevalent in most parts of Orissa, with modernisation and consumerism only altering the orientation of the practice. Where animal sacrifice was a community affair in the old days, meant for the general welfare of the village, people now indulge in it to pander to their individual desires.

According to law secretary H Mohapatra, although the Cruelty to Animals (Prevention) Act prohibits animal sacrifice, the law is not being implemented effectively. The apparent fear is "offending people's sentiments", in the words of a police officer.

Butt Beauty

No Ifs and Buts for the Perfect Male Butt

Men have always been fond of women's posteriors. But did you know that women are equally fond of men's butts? And that's no laughing matter, if you speak to Vimal Malik, a surgeon at Eleganza Rejuvenation Clinic. Malik reveals that there is an "influx of men who want treatment for butt reduction".

For every 10 women walking in for some treatment or the other, there are three men. And liposuction for the butt is commonly asked for, according to Malik.

A Delhi cosmetologist claims that a businessman came all the way from Jabalpur to have his posterior reshaped. And cosmetologists in the Capital city say that even foreign clients turn up asking for butt treatments.

Another cosmetic surgeon reveals that more than overweight men, it is the young lads who want a nip or two in the right places to get a perfect backside.

Corporate Buzz

The Origins of BPL

Do you know what the electronic goods company BPL's full name denotes? It stands for British Physical Laboratories. Can you guess which of these countries the company originated from: Japan, Britain, USA or France?

If you said yes to any of the four countries, including Britain, you are off the mark. Despite its misleading name, British Physical Laboratories is an Indian company, based in Palakkad, Kerala. Founded by TPG Nambiar in 1963, the company initially manufactured hermetically sealed precision panel meters. From 1980 onwards, BPL began manufacturing televisions and telecom equipment.

The only foreign connection BPL has is its international tie-ups and the fact that Nambiar worked in the UK and the USA, before coming back to India with the dream of setting up his own electronic products company that would one day be a household name. Today, BPL is one of India's biggest consumer electronics company.

Mobile Phones Zoom Ahead

On 20 January 2003 BSNL Chairman Prithpal Singh revealed that while landline phones received 243 million subscribers in 100 years, *the world saw 276 mobile phone users within just three years!*

Career Conundrums

Kerala's Over-qualified Unemployed

In November 2002, when the Lal Bahadur Shastri Institute (a public education institution), Thiruvananthapuram, checked the responses for some temporary clerical posts, it received a few surprises. Amongst the 13,500 applicants, there were two doctors and 20 engineers!

The posts (eight lower division clerks, eight peons and one typist) had been advertised a few months earlier. From these 13,500 applicants, 5,000 were highly qualified. There were even post-graduates and those with diplomas in computer engineering. Although the practice has been to disallow overqualified candidates, a recent court order has made it mandatory for an employer to test each applicant.

Amongst the 7,000 applicants for LD clerks, there were two with MBBS degrees, one of them already serving at a primary health centre in Kozhikode. Although the posts were not even permanent ones, 20 B.Tech graduates had also applied for the clerical posts, where the emoluments are Rs.5,000 per month.

Celebrity Capers

Fake Husain Foxes Husain!

You would be able to recognise your own work, wouldn't you? Perhaps not, if one goes by the experience of Maqbool Fida Husain. It seems that in December 2002, MF Husain found himself in a ticklish situation where he failed to spot some fake Husains, instead vouchsafing for their authenticity!

A lady Mumbai art dealer is said to have asked Husain*saab* to check some paintings and let her know whether they were his works so that she could buy them. According to Husain the works were such "excellent copies" that he thought they were his own work! The first painting was a watercolour, Marwari Couple, the second a set of bulls and the third a canvas of a scene from Kolkata.

The 87-year-old maestro inspected the works and didn't find anything amiss. Only when Husain visited Kolkata and met his friend, tennis player Naresh Kumar, who owns quite a few Husains, that he saw the original Marwari Couple on Kumar's living room wall, much to his surprise.

Naresh Kumar was in turn surprised when Husain mentioned he had seen the same painting in Mumbai recently. Naresh and his wife Sunita were reportedly stumped about this, since they wondered where the forgers had obtained a copy of the original to make a copy, as the painting had never left their possession after it was acquired.

Back in Mumbai, Husain told the lady dealer (who has been in the business for 20 years) that the paintings in her possession were fake. Although Husain claimed he'd not had a close look at the paintings, the art dealer says that Husain*saab* "examined the paintings minutely and told me categorically that they were his works". The lady claims she even questioned him about when he had painted these watercolours, since they were "quite different from his trademark style".

Thanks to Husain's response: "*Ye mera kaam hai*", the lady purchased the paintings. With Husain later telling her that the paintings were forgeries, the art dealer was said to have sent the paintings back to Husain to ensure he could decide about the authenticity after a second close look.

As for the master, Husain says he has no intentions of filing a complaint about the forgeries.

The Maharaja and His Toy Train

Here's a Maharaja who wants his toy back! And he'll have his way, for a change. We are referring to Maharaja Ranjitsinh Gaekwad of Baroda, who has asked the Vadodara Municipal Corporation (VMC) to return the toy train gifted to him by his father on his fifth birthday.

The VMC had used the train for years to take children on joy rides in Kamatibaug. In January 2003, the VMC's general board decided the locomotive should be returned to its rightful owner, the Maharaja.

Naturally, Maharaja Ranjitsinh was overjoyed on hearing the news that his toy was being returned to him! In the words of the Maharaja: "There are so many sweet memories attached to this locomotive. I still remember my father Pratapsinh Gaekwad playing the ticket-seller when we went for a ride."

The Maharaja also remembers his father sitting in a cabin at the station and stamping the tickets for him and his siblings. The sentimental ties towards the toy locomotive have definitely not diminished a whit over the years.

Manoj Kumar the Homeopath

Everyone surely knows Manoj Kumar is an actor and film-maker. Before Manoj Kumar made it big, he worked as a ghostwriter at various studios, earning Rs.11 per scene. Few will know that Manoj Kumar is a homeopath too.

In an interview published in the *Sunday Times of India*, the film-maker revealed: "...I fulfilled my mother's dream by becoming a homeopath. I was introduced to this form of medicine by Ashok Kumar while shooting for *Grihasthi*. Noticing warts on my cheek, he put me under homeopathic treatment and I was cured within a week. Subsequently, I learnt and practised homeopathy and run a charitable clinic today."

From amongst those Manoj Kumar prescribes medicine too are Union Minister Lal Krishna Advani and actor-MP Shatrughan Sinha. The latter, incidentally, had once run Manoj down in an article titled *Roti, Kapda Aur Bewra*. Manoj Kumar refutes rumours that he is an alcoholic. "I maintain I am a teetotaller who indulges himself very rarely. I am addicted to herbal tea and smoke two cigarettes a day. I am a workaholic, but certainly not an alcoholic."

No Accolades for Tenzing Norgay

You would think somebody who planted his country's flag atop Mount Everest would have received accolades and awards in his country. Perhaps - and perhaps not...

Sherpa Tenzing Norgay's case is a classic one. Fifty years after Tenzing planted Nepal's standard atop the world's highest peak, the Nepalese Government is unwilling to honour him posthumously simply because he had subsequently acquired Indian citizenship. However, to mark the golden jubilee of the Everest ascent, the Nepalese Government conferred honorary citizenship on Sir Edmund Hillary on 29 May 2003.

Tenzing grew up in Nepal and spent his early years tending his father's yak herds on high mountain passes below Mount Everest. In his teens, he migrated to India seeking work. In Darjeeling, he worked as a porter on several pioneering pre-war British expeditions to the Himalayas.

He shot into the limelight and wrote his name into the record books when he scaled Mt Everest along with New Zealand's Edmund Hillary on 29 May 1953. The Nepal Government had then hailed the achievement as its own and he was quickly awarded the Nepal Tara (Star of Nepal) medal.

Soon after this, then Indian Prime Minister Jawaharlal Nehru gave him an Indian passport so that he could travel to England. Tenzing Norgay accepted the Indian passport – and inadvertently rubbed his countrymen the wrong way. Thereafter, Tenzing spent most of his life in India.

The Nepal Mountaineering Association wants Tenzing to be made a *Rashtriya Vibhuti* – a honour reserved for the kingdom's elite dead – but the Nepal Government will seemingly not entertain this suggestion. A previous Indian recipient was Gautam Buddha, who was born in the border town of Lumbini that today falls within the borders of Nepal.

City Tales

Golden Temple the Best, Not Taj Mahal

For those who thought Agra with its Taj Mahal was the best tourist puller, here's news. According to a British survey, the Golden Temple in Amritsar ranks sixth amongst the 50 best sites in the world that people would "die to see". And the Taj Mahal comes 10th in the survey. India's other landmark, Mount Everest, comes in at number 30.

Travel agents in London say that the maximum number of tourists make bookings to India to see the Golden Temple and the Taj Mahal. Over 20,000 people were interviewed for the survey, which was commissioned for screening in the British Broadcasting Corporation's *Holiday* programme. Tour operators were themselves surprised that the Golden Temple beat the Taj Mahal in the rankings.

Incidentally, the world's number one spot was America's Grand Canyon, followed by Australia's Great Barrier Reef, Florida's Walt Disney World, New Zealand's South Island and South Africa's Cape Town. The seventh, eighth and ninth spots were held by the gamblers' paradise Las Vegas, the city of harbours, Sydney and the city of skyscrapers, New York.

Kolkata's History Dates 2,000 Years, Not 300

It is generally believed that the British founded Kolkata just 300 years ago. British trader Job Charnock is crediting for "discovering" Kolkata on 24 August 1690.

There are many who contest these claims. Says Mayor Subrata Mukherjee: "The name Kolkata finds mention in documents dated much before 24 August 1690. The name occurs in documents like *Chandimangal*, which was written between 1598 and 1606." Indeed, an aristocratic Bengali family that once owned a major part of the city has challenged the city's birthday and history in court, with the court ruling in their favour in May 2003.

In January 2003, archaeologists buttressed these arguments when they stumbled upon an urban settlement that dates back to the second century BC. On the northern outskirts of the city near Dum Dum, archaeologists have discovered artefacts and "habitational deposits" that were probably used in this urban settlement.

Experts from the Archaeological Survey of India (ASI) say that the artefacts, potshards and seals seem to be from the Sunga Kusana period. ASI superintendent archaeologist Bimal Bandopadhyay said the indications were that an urban population lived in the area for centuries. The cause of the settlement dying out is yet to be ascertained.

Besides the artefacts and other items, human skulls were also recovered, which were sent for laboratory tests. Scientists expressed confidence that the human remains were at least 2,000 years old. If proved true, it will bury yet another Western myth.

World's Greenest Capital City

Which is the capital of Gujarat? Did you say Ahmedabad? No! Despite the popular misconception, Gandhinagar is the capital of Gujarat.

There is another noteworthy fact about Gandhinagar - it is the world's greenest city. A few years ago, a worldwide survey adjudged Islamabad as the world's greenest national capital, with 325 trees per hectare. But purely as a state capital, Gandhinagar actually beats Islamabad's record by a wide margin, since it has 425 trees per hectare.

The other statistics: with 32 lakh trees for a population of just 1.5 lakh people that's 22 trees per person! Spread over 56 square kilometres, there are 35 species of trees, including neem, mahua, banyan, pipal and gulmohar. This may be the only Indian city with more trees than people!

Mumbai's Incredible *Dabbawallas*

These men do Mumbai proud. And with just one error in eight million tasks, who wouldn't! In September 2002, Gangaram Talekar and Raghunath Medge, secretary and president of the Nutan Mumbai Tiffin Box Suppliers were invited to the CII Leadership Summit for their presentation. As Talekar spoke in his *Mumbaiya* Hindi, talking about how his *dhanda* worked, bosses of corporate India listened raptly.

Not surprisingly, these men didn't know about Six Sigma (a global efficiency standard denoting only 3.4 mistakes in a million tasks) until Talekar's company achieved it. Talekar disclosed that his men only made an error in eight million deliveries. This was a fact that he also told *Forbes* magazine, when they visited him. "We may make a mistake, but never mistakes," Talekar states proudly.

The 120-year-old organisation has a system that works with clockwork precision. Daily, 200,000 tiffin boxes are delivered and taken back with the help of 5,000 bicycle deliverymen. Beginning at 9:30 AM, they have just three hours to do this, for which they also thank the local trains in Mumbai.

What can corporate India learn from this? A lot. For instance, just how the system ticks. Each group leader himself goes through the system and knows how it works. The system of coding is straight and uncomplicated. A new *dabbawalla* is inducted after just two days of learning the job. Each person is responsible for his own welfare and his bread and butter. So there are no sulks and no strikes.

Any wonder that Star Plus, Proctor & Gamble and Hindustan Lever are already advertising on their *dabbas*?

Mumbai Colony Leads TV-free Life

While Americans are just beginning to realise the importance of No-TV days, residents from a Mumbai suburb have been leading no-TV lifestyles for many years.

It all began in the 1990s, when Ali Muhammed Dawa from Jogeshwari, Mumbai, actually flung his television set out of his balcony. Populated by members of the minority community in Jogeshwari West, this colony near the Railway Station has been leading a TV-free lifestyle for over a decade.

Today, these residents find more time for one another and their children. Nor are they saddled with numerous problems that couch potatoes develop over the years, after hours of incessant TV viewing.

As Delhi Traffic Crawls, Cycles May Run Faster

As we all know, Delhi has the most vehicular traffic (3.7 million in 2002), even more than the combined numbers of Mumbai, Kolkata and Chennai. Average traffic speeds have currently plummeted to bullock cart speed, 15 kmph. Idling time at traffic signals has increased to a minimum of five minutes during peak hours. And peak hours now mean three hours in the morning (8:30 to 11:30 AM) and three hours in the evening (4:30 to 7:30 PM).

To make matters worse, 500 new vehicles are on the roads every day. Furthermore, 100,000 vehicles from the neighbouring states also ply on the Capital's roads. Every third person in Delhi now owns a car or a two-wheeler, which is way ahead of the national average.

If things continue in this manner, by 2010 cycles will be a faster mode of transport in Delhi than cars!

Ancient Water Bodies for Water-harvesting

India may have some of the highest rainfall levels in the world, yet we are perennially short of water. Since its founding in 1948, Israel may have the least rainfall level, but this Jewish nation has shown it has a green thumb and become self-sufficient in water through sensible water conservation and water-harvesting techniques.

While Israel has used the most modern techniques to augment its water resources, believe it or not, India will be tapping its medieval water bodies to achieve self-sufficiency in water. Moves in this direction have already been made in Delhi. The Union Water Resource Ministry has instructed the Central Ground Water Board (CGWB) to look into the potential for recharging water levels through *baolis* (step-wells). News reports indicate that the CGWB has identified 13 *baolis* throughout the city, besides four water bodies like Neela Hauz and Hauz-e-Shamsi. The step-wells include *Agrasen*, *Gandhak* and *Rajon ki baolis*.

Officials told the media that they would study which of the structures still have a recharge potential, besides looking into the hydro-geological pattern of the area in which the *baolis* are located. With *baolis* that have the potential, the Board will then check out how modern technology can be used to enhance the effectiveness of these medieval water bodies.

The current *Dilli Sarkar* is not the first one to try looking to the past for a better future. In the 14th century, the eccentric Delhi ruler Firoz Shah Tughlaq desilted the Hauz Khas water structure, which was first built by Alauddin Khilji, in 1295, for the residents of Siri. This later fell into disuse, until Tughlaq revived it a century later.

In January 2002, the Archaeological Survey of India had met with some success when it had worked on *Agrasen ki baoli*, which lies on Hailey Road. After the ASI had cleared debris up to three metres and bricks from a few places had fallen off, groundwater began gushing into the disused *baoli*.

For many towns and cities, adequate water resources could literally mean a question of life and death, for history tells us that Fatehpur Sikri was abandoned due to the paucity of water.

Using Baolis, British *Ishtyle*

Baolis were originally meant to store water. But trust the Brits to come up with a novel and nefarious way of using *baolis*. Thanks to its efforts in desilting a 14th century *baoli* in the Red Fort, the ASI stumbled upon a step-well that was used by the British to house prisoners facing the historical Indian National Army trial.

The British used the step-well as a makeshift prison by blocking the open chambers with iron bricks and leaving a small opening only for the prisoners to breathe. The Brits further defiled the ancient structure with other chambers being blocked with iron grills and a toilet having been constructed for prisoners inside the *baoli* itself. Incidentally, this Red Fort *baoli* predates the Fort, which was constructed in the 17th century.

Book a Tramcar for Your Marriage

People in Kolkata have another way to celebrate their parties and wedding functions – inside trams! Calcutta Tramways Company (CTC) has been looking at new means to augment its depleted coffers and has hit upon the novel idea of hiring out tramcars for special occasions.

In February 2003, the CTC's heritage tramcar, Banalata, with its well maintained and plush seats was hired by a wedding party to take the bride, the groom and other family members to the groom's residence after the wedding. In January too, the tramcar had been given on hire. On each occasion, the tramcar earned more than five times the money it would have earned from a regulation return trip.

The enthusiastic response has emboldened the CTC to decide to make this a permanent business venture. While CTC currently earns Rs.1,500 and Rs.2,000 per round trip for the trams, it charges Rs.10,000 for the special two and a half hour ride. The tramcar has to be booked 10 days in advance.

Flyover Repairs at Twice the Construction Costs

The New Delhi Municipal Council (NDMC) first uses substandard material to construct a flyover. That done, in the subsequent years it keeps spending hefty sums to repair its own faulty construction... again and again and again.

Consider the School Lane Flyover opposite Lalit Suri's Intercontinental Hotel, constructed in 1982 at a cost of Rs.3.3 crore. In the 20 years since then, the NDMC has spent more than twice this amount in rectifying the faulty construction. Officials reveal that the outdated rocker roller technology was used instead of the superior Neoprene technology. The latter technology was used for the flyover opposite the Oberoi Hotel and hasn't had any recurring problems. But the School Lane Flyover first developed problems in 1989 that consumed Rs.40 lakh to repair.

Thereafter, the problem keeps recurring, guzzling bigger and bigger amounts. But somewhere, somebody must surely be making a cool packet, thanks to the regular repairs.

Whispering Room for Lovers in Kolkata Museum

Scientists at the Birla Institute and Technological Museum in Kolkata have designed a balloon-shaped room for lovers, where they can exchange sweet nothings without being overheard by others.

The room's acoustics ensure that a person can whisper and still be heard clearly by a partner. Up to 15 persons can sit together in the room and talk to their partners without being overheard by anybody else.

Cricket Jazz

Name Games

Want to make some "easy" money? Here's your chance. An Australian magazine is offering Australian $5 if you can pronounce the name of Sri Lankan pace bowler Chaminda Vaas.

Cakewalk, isn't it? Not really! That's because Chaminda's full name is Warnakulasuriya Patabendige Ushantha Joseph Chaminda Vaas!

What? You didn't get the name? Hell, don't ask us to repeat it! The trouble isn't worth Australian $5!

What's in a Name?

Talking about names, there are some communities where siblings in the same family use different full names. For instance, this writer himself knew three Muslim brothers who had different "surnames". The eldest brother was Abdul Wahab (he is no more), the middle one is Kaleem Sheikh and the third brother is Aleem Aziz.

The world of cricket goes one better on siblings with different surnames. The 2003 World Cup in South Africa featured a Kenyan player who went by a different surname on different days, depending on whether he fancied his tribe or his village on a particular day! The player in question is the Kenyan opener Kennedy who goes by the surnames Obuya (the name of his tribe) or Otieno (the name of his village).

So don't be confused if in some matches the Kenyan opener calls himself Kennedy Obuya and in others he is Kennedy Otieno. You could simply refer to him as Kennedy O!

India and the World's Richest Cricketer

Just a decade ago, it would have seemed impossible that any cricketer could be amongst the richest Indians. But today, India's national cricketing icon, Sachin Tendulkar, has achieved just that. UK publication *Eastern Eye* has compiled a list of the 20 richest Indians, which includes Tendulkar at number 18.

Wipro's Azim Premji heads the list with an estimated wealth of Rs.17,600 crore. The listing:

Name/Company-Occupation	Worth (Rs. Crore)
1. Azim Premji/Wipro	17,600
2. Shiv Nadir/HCL	6,900
3. Mukesh-Anil Ambani/Reliance	5,000
4. NR Narayana Murthy/Infosys	4,700
5. Malvinder-Shivendra Singh/Ranbaxy	2,500
6. Rahul Bajaj	2,500
7. Subhash Chandra/Zee TV	2,200
8. Kumarmangalam Birla	2,100
9. The Hindujas	1,800
10. RC Burman/Dabur	1,800
11. B Ramalinga Raju/Satyam Computers	1,600
12. Vijay Mallya/UB Breweries	600
13. Gautam Singhania/Raymonds	600
14. Shahnaz Hussain/Beauty czarina	400
15. Niranjan Hiranandani/Real estate developer	400
16. Anu Aga/Thermax	300
17. Amitabh Bachchan/Film-star	200
18. **Sachin Tendulkar**/Cricketer	200
19. Naina Kidwai/HSBC	170
20. Sapoorji Pallonji/Entrepreneur	100

Sachin and Sehwag's Lookalikes

Some guys can go places just because of their faces – Jeevan Sharma and Balbir Chand from Ludhiana fall into this category. Sharma – who happens to be a cutter in a hosiery unit – looks like Virender Sehwag, while Chand is a lookalike of Sachin Tendulkar.

Thanks to their looks, Pakistani-singer-popular-in-India Adnan Sami has featured them on his video. Sharma has also received offers from the Bunny and Zone advertisement company of MTV, besides a call from Bollywood.

Not surprisingly, Sharma has begun learning to walk, talk and behave like Sehwag. Now all that the duo have to do is learn to bat like Virender Sehwag and Sachin Tendulkar and bowlers of the world will have double nightmares.

Crime Beat

Passports and the Criminal Pecking Order

If you don't know who's who in the pecking order of the Crime Syndicate, here's news... Dons like Dawood Ibrahim and pretenders like Aftab Ansari are set apart by the number of fake passports they hold.

Accordingly, Aftab Ansari has just two fake passports. Dawood's right-hand man Chhota Shakeel has six. Dawood's *jaani dushman* Chhota Rajan has eight. Abu Salem (who is currently cooling his heels behind bars in Lisbon, Portugal with his moll, Monica Bedi) has 12. As for the big daddy of them all, Dawood has 20 fake passports, all issued from Mumbai.

So these fake passports aren't just passports to crime, they are also passports to criminal hierarchy.

Crop News

Neem Makes Diseased Tree Give Record Mangoes

What would you do if your mango yielded only trouble instead of fruits for 14 years? You'd most likely wield the axe! But HK Lakshman Rao was emotionally attached to the tree, so he used his grey cells instead and is reaping rich dividends since then.

Rao's Badami mango tree had been infertile for 14 years before Rao decided to give his tree a "complete neem treatment". The move paid rich dividends and in May 2002 the tree gave a bountiful harvest of golden Badami mangoes.

For nearly a decade and a half, the tree had only yielded 100 to 150 rotten fruits every year. But on 2 May 2002, Rao plucked 2,085 ripe and delicious Badami mangoes. This bounty harvest attracted all the more attention from agro-scientists as the country's mango crop is said to have failed in 2002.

Lakshman Rao reveals that he had brought the mango sapling from Mysore. In the beginning itself, it turned out to be diseased and was infested with insects. Rao tried several types of fertilisers and insecticides, yet nothing worked. On many occasions, he or the family members felt like chopping the tree. His emotions, however, prevented this drastic step. And then he hit upon the neem treatment idea.

When the last harvest was over in June, he trimmed the tree. Next, he buried a mixture of dried neem leaves, five kilos of neem cake and sand in a moat that was 1.5 feet deep, which he'd dug around the tree's roots. To maintain the moisture level, the tree was watered intermittently. In place of chemical pesticides, he used neem oil diluted in warm water. The warm liquid was then sprayed over the tree thrice a year in the months of July, October and January.

Pretty soon, the results were there to see. The tree began looking healthy, the flowers stopped falling and each flower bloomed into a fruit. And the fruits had now stopped falling before they had ripened.

Rao says the neem treatment idea came to him when he was on a visit to Daboli near Mumbai, where he had taken his students (Rao is a management consultant) to an estate for a workshop on rural marketing of Ratnagiri mangoes. This was when he picked up some tips on the use of the neem cake. However, while neem cake was being used partly in Daboli, he employed a complete treatment.

Since the news of the bumper harvest hit the headlines, over 150 people have visited Rao's house for a *dekko* at the tree. In Chennai itself, Rao says, there are four lakh mango trees. Just imagine the record harvest if neem treatment was given to each of these trees!

Music Therapy Spurs Crop Growth

Are falling crop yields bothering you? Forget chemical fertilisers. And while you're welcome to try organic farming, you could also check out Music Therapy. Serious!

Farmers in the Krishna district of Andhra Pradesh have been doing just that - and reaping a bountiful harvest in the bargain. Sugarcane yields in Vuyyur and Laxmipuram areas have increased by nearly six to eight tonnes per acre after the farmers began playing music to their plants. Crops in nearby farms that are not subjected to sonic treatment yield an average of 33 tonnes per acre, while those crops that "listen" to music daily yield an average of 38 to 42 tonnes per acre, a record yield in AP. In monetary terms, this increased yield results in additional revenues of Rs.5,400 to Rs.7,200 (@ Rs.900 per tonne) for farmers.

That isn't all. The daily crop of plants has also shown substantial increase. Agronomists from IIT, Chennai studied the crop growth in treated and untreated fields and found that plant growth was twice as much in the former.

Music therapy for plants is not such a bother, too. The farmers simply hoist a tape recorder above the crops with the help of a bamboo pole, exposing their plants to half-an-hour of music twice a day. Plants are said to have a "ear" for all kinds of music - classical, western and even Indipop. The actual results vary from plant to plant, depending on the music and the frequency of play.

This musical venture began in 1997-98 when the local KCP Sugar Industries decided to revive the "sonic treatment" experiment started by its former chairman, B Maruthi Rao. Inspired by the principles pioneered by India's famous scientist, Jagadish Chandra Bose, Rao conducted experiments with crops, proving that plant health and yield could be enhanced by playing music to them regularly. Experimenting with various forms of music initially, Rao finally selected a kind of staccato instrumental music that seems very harsh to human ears, but promotes the maximum growth in sugarcane.

Encouraged by the early results, the company then began handing out cassette players and music tapes to the farmers, motivating more of them to try the sonic treatment.

Before this, an eminent Pune musicologist and Ayurvaid, Pandurang Shastri Deshpande, is also said to have discovered that Hindustani classical music had a soothing effect on his plants, just like it did on his patients. Dr Deshpande is said to have played records of *Raag Bhairavi*, in the voice of nine different singers, before nine potted touch-me-not plants for a month daily.

The results were said to be eye-opening. The plant that was exposed to Abdul Karim Khan's *Bhairavi* grew an amazing 430 per cent! Dr Deshpande's articles on the subject were subsequently published in a book, *Smruti Grantha,* released in August 2002 by Pandit Bhimsen Joshi.

Although music therapy is now an accepted discipline in the West with quite a few courses and practitioners, the Medical Council of India still retains a strong dose of scepticism regarding this therapy's curative aspects. But don't wait folks - check out music therapy first hand. For yourself... and your plants!

The Ever-green Mango Tree

Most trees flower in the season that Nature allotted them. Not so with Bholanath Jha's mango tree. The owner of Jhapaha Farms, this man from Muzaffarpur has a Barahmasia mango tree in his garden that faithfully delivers fruits 365 days of the year.

What's the trick with this tree, you may wonder. Simple! Jha's tree has the specialty of having branches that bear fruit in different stages at the same time. For instance, one branch could just be flowering, while another could be at the midway stage and a third branch could be bearing ripened fruit! Look at the tree throughout the year and you will find some branches filled with flowers - while others are heavily laden with ripe mangoes.

According to Jha, the mangoes that ripen in the months of June and July are the best. Besides, the harvest is bountiful if the farm is ploughed right after the main season, irrigated when no major flowering is in process and if fertilisers are given twice or thrice a year.

Record Yields Bring Harvest of Misery

Sometimes, more is definitely less! This is a lesson that farmers in Kharupetia, Assam, learnt in December 2002. Thousands of farmers are badly hit because of record crop outputs.

Fifty-year-old Moinuddin Ahmed was riding his bullock cart home with tear-filled eyes as he returned from the wholesale market in Kharupetia village, some 70 km north of Guwahati. Ahmed reveals that he had loaded his bullock cart with cabbages before sunrise, reaching the market early in the morning. But there were scarcely any buyers and the prices fell to abysmal levels.

Even when Ahmed offered to sell his cabbages for 25 paise a kilo, there were still no buyers. Distraught, Ahmed dumped over 100 kg of cabbages down the drain.

Tomatoes or cauliflower were selling for less than 50 paise a kilo in the wholesale market. Ahmed moans that with months of hard labour and money down the drain, he feels like committing suicide. Indeed, three years ago, at least a dozen tomato farmers committed suicide in Assam after a similar crash in prices triggered by surplus production.

Is there a way out of this surplus imbroglio? Yes, says Ardhendu Dey, the agriculture minister. The minister reveals that vegetable production has shot up manifold as farmers are using high-yield varieties supplied by the government. Not to mention the advanced training imparted by experts to the farmers. The government had been motivating the farmers to change their pattern of cultivation and grow other crops, like pulses and oilseeds, as these earn higher returns. The farmers, however, insisted on cultivating the same vegetables, leading to the glut, claims the minister. With the crash in prices in December 2002, perhaps the farmers will not repeat their mistake this time around.

Customs & Traditions

Apatani Women Wear Nose Plugs to Look Ugly

The Apatanis are a tribe in Arunachal Pradesh who still regard the Sun and Moon as their gods, despite the spread of Christianity in the state. Witch doctors serve as links with their gods. The witch doctor conducts all rituals and sacrifices after examining a chicken liver.

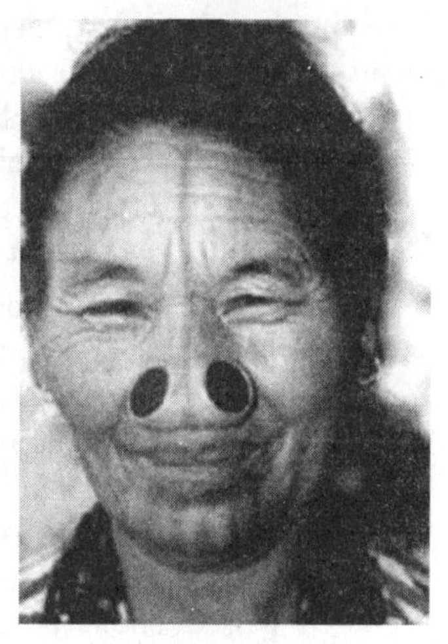

The Apatanis don't waste their hard-earned wealth in building religious monuments. Prayers can be offered at any place and at any time. And to construct a religious structure, all that is required is building an altar out of bamboo.

The majority of Apatani women still continue to wear nose plugs, which make them look unattractive to members of other tribes!

The death of an old Apatani is cause for celebration, where singing and dancing is followed by the exchange of presents. These gifts are then buried along with the dead person, since the Apatanis believe the dead can enjoy these in their next life.

Garbas without Girls

Navratri conjures images of gaily-bedecked girls dancing to the tune of drums. But Shahpur and Vadodara in Gujarat, the land of garbas, have a different tale to tell.

Take the 175-year-old garba that's held at Sadhumata ni Pol in Shahpur, where women play second fiddle to the men-folk during the eight-day garba festival. Here, men don ornamented *lehanga-cholis* and wigs in order to swing with gay abandon to the drumbeats. According to a local resident, it all started as a ritual to "please Sadhumata and free the community from all curses".

At Amba Mata ni Pol in Vadodara, too, garbas are an exclusive male event. Here, the no-women garba tradition goes back over 200 years. Local resident Virendra Shah says that while there is no rule that debars women from participating, it has traditionally been only the men who take part in the garba. Most of the men are said to be devotees who come from far-off places.

Old Vadodara, however, takes the cake when it comes to breaking tradition. Here, neither men nor women have exclusive rights on the garba! Instead, it is eunuchs who observe a peculiar tradition of garba, which includes observing a fast and performing *havan* (a special puja for the fire god, Agni).

No Brides in Haryana – Grooms go Abegging

For decades, Haryana was one of the states notorious for female foeticide. The chickens have finally come home to roost, though. Young men looking for prospective brides have to hunt high and low. There are apparently no brides available within reach. Haryanvis looking to wed are being forced to buy girls from neighbouring states like Bihar, Madhya Pradesh and West Bengal. The sums range between Rs.20,000 and Rs.30,000. These girls are then passed off as members of their own caste.

The 2001 Census tells its own tale of the notorious districts with a lopsided sex ratio in the 0–6 age group: Kurukshetra (770:1,000), Sonepat (783:1,000), Ambala (784:1,000) and Rohtak (796:1,000).

Dr Richa Tanwar, director, Women's Studies, Kurukshetra University, says the situation will get worse in the years ahead, as the sex ratio amongst the literate has dipped to 618 girls to 1,000 boys!

For the Haryana villagers, finding a bride is not the only problem. Convincing the villagers that the 'outsiders' are from their *biradari* is just as important. As long as the girl is not from a schedule caste or schedule tribe, the panchayats are willing to turn a blind eye. Boys desperate to marry are even willing to wed girls from lower or backward castes, although SC/ ST girls are still avoided.

Incredibly, panchayat member Rami Ratri says: "Polygamy is common in Haryana; men will marry twice and thrice to get a male child. But I won't be surprised if, due to the shortage of brides, families revert to the earlier practice of polyandry where one bride was shared by the male members of a family."

Sadly, fewer women do not mean the women are now calling the shots. Just the opposite is true. Says Manisha, associate programme coordinator for the government-funded Population and Development Education Programme: "Having fewer women does not mean the premium on them increases. On the contrary, they are being subjected to more violence and families are being forced to keep them cloistered in their homes."

It looks like some men will never learn... until the laws of Nature teach them another lesson or two.

Food Facts

Gourmet Tales

Did you know that the first tandoori chicken was prepared in Lahore, some time between World War I and the partition of India in 1947? Did you also know that the first *medu vada* was made in Meddur, a town in Karnataka?

A food critic who writes for the *Hindustan Times* under the strange pseudonym, Grand Fromage, has uncovered these strange food facts.

Smells like Shit but Tastes like Heaven!

Did you know that there is a fruit that smells like shit but tastes like heaven? Yes, it's true. The fruit in question is the durian that is sold in south-east Asian markets, despite its disgusting smell.

The stink of the durian ("stink" is indeed the right word) has been described as "the smell of old socks", "like papaya fermented after a fruit-eating bat has peed on it", "like a dead rat decomposing in a plate of vomit" and plain old "shit"!

Strangely, those who swear by the taste of the durian describe it as: "tastes like heaven" or "a rich butter-like custard highly flavoured with almonds". But who would eat something that smells like crap defies the imagination!

Wax-coated Produce

Have you wondered how the local fruit vendor sells apples that seem fresher and redder than ever before? Or how the vegetable vendor has produce that is greener than in the good old days?

A report in *Star News* blows the lid off these "fresh" fruits and vegetables. Believe it or not, vendors have taken to coating their produce with wax! Vendors claim that pests destroy up to 30 to 40 per cent of their fruits and vegetables and the wax coat ensures the produce remains fresh and unaffected for longer periods. Not to mention, imparting the produce a shiny, fresh and richly coloured look!

The Health Ministry has already taken note of the unsavoury practice. Although the wax is food-grade material imported from the United States and Europe, the authorities have expressed alarm at the wax coating of produce because of the Indian vendors' penchant for adulterating every item that passes through their hands. Adulteration adds to their profit margins, although what it does to the bellies of customers hardly bothers the adulterators.

Hopefully, it should not be long before the authorities ban the wax coating of food produce.

Indian Chocolates Have Minimal Cocoa

You know that cocoa is used to make chocolates, don't you? But did you know that Indian chocolates, even some of the expensive ones, have very little cocoa? Aha! So now you know why foreign chocolates taste so much better - because these actually have cocoa.

Indian brands use more of the wafer content of cocoa to give that chocolaty taste, and this includes popular brands like *5 Star* or *Perk*. And chocolate heavyweight Cadbury plans to reduce the amount of cocoa even more and add more wafer, thanks to the ongoing war in the Ivory Coast, the world's largest producer of cocoa, that's hampering production.

Food Aid for Starving Afghans

While many poor people may be dying of starvation in some states of India, the country has a surplus of food grain stocks. Thanks to this, India is willing to contribute between one and two per cent of this surplus stock to help feed the hungry in other parts of the world.

On a visit to India in December 2002, James Morrison, Executive Director of the United Nations World Food Programme, met Agriculture Minister Ajit Singh and praised the country for the food aid provided to Afghanistan. In India, he had sought the Indian Government's help in feeding the large number of people in Afghanistan who have had some of the toughest years in recent times due to the prolonged national conflict and drought.

While the government should be lauded for helping the Afghans, will something be done to feed starving Indians? Thanks to the abysmal Public Distribution System, which has collapsed, while there is a surplus of food grains, the country is unable to distribute this where it is most required.

Pune's Parantha Festival

You may have heard of mango festivals and food festivals celebrating a particular state or country's cuisine. But Pune did things differently - it held a *Parantha* festival!

This retired officers' paradise made news when an international *parantha* festival was held here between October 23 and 27 by the Nagpur-based Manohar Group. During the festival, 60 varieties of *paranthas* from India, Afghanistan, Russia and the Gulf countries tickled the palates of food lovers, according to the convenor and chief chef Vishnu Manohar.

There were 13 types of *paranthas* from Maharashtra, besides others from Gujarat, Rajasthan, Madhya Pradesh, Kerala and Chhattisgarh. Chefs from the Gulf were said to have specially flown down to prepare *barkhaani parantha, Dubai da parantha, Kabuli, khamiri roti, khamboos, moongai,* stuffed *naan* and *lasani naan*, amongst other mouth-watering *paranthas*. The paranthas were reasonably priced between Rs.15 and Rs.30.

Chatni, raita, subzi, dal and fresh butter were also served to go with the piping hot *paranthas*. Stuffed *tawa paranthas, chhole bhature, makke di roti, sarson da saag* and mixed fruit *parantha* were also available. A giant five-foot-wide *parantha* was specially prepared for the festival using eight kilos of flour.

Government Machinations

Kerala Gambles to Fill Empty Coffers

Like some north Indian states, the Kerala treasury is empty. To pull itself out of the red, the state is willing to gamble on a lottery ticket and officials are now saddled with the task of selling Kerala's Akshaya lottery tickets.

If a person visits a government office, while he is uncertain of his work being done, he can be certain of having to part with Rs.100-200, all for some colourful lottery tickets. Officials claim the instructions have come from no less than the Chief Minister's Office.

Officials claim they've never had to work so hard! A panchayat employee at Nedumangad said he was given a "bunch of 500 tickets", of which he had managed to sell 150 only. As for the balance, "it looks like I will have to foot the bill". The government's thinking is simple - a ticket distributed is a ticket sold!

Senior officials find it easier to foot the bill, rather than attempt selling the tickets. The present lottery idea is said to have arisen from the sheer financial distress Kerala is currently undergoing.

Even Beggars Rejecting Small Change in TN

The Government has not yet demonetised *chiller*, but going by what's happening in Tiruchirappalli, Tamil Nadu, you'd swear it had. With rumours being rife that coins of lower denomination have been demonetised, people in Tamil Nadu's southern districts are refusing to treat five paise, 10 paise and

20 paise coins as legal tender. Some traders are consequently disposing of these coins as scrap.

News reports indicate that bags of rejected coins are piling up at transport corporations. Traders are at a loss as to how the rumours gained currency that these coins are no longer legal tender. Says a trader, Chandra Naidu: "At one point, the coins started accumulating so much that some merchants themselves could have spread the rumour."

That's not all. Reports indicate that even beggars have become choosers and are refusing to accept such coins at some places! Private traders are said to be selling bags of coins to scrap metal dealers. Over 200 scrap dealers are reportedly involved in buying coins for their metal value.

Health Travails

Use Cow Dung for Protection Against Radiation

While companies in the West may come out with various sun protection creams that cost millions to develop, the Uttar Pradesh Gau Seva Ayog claims there is a much cheaper and easier way of protection against the harmful radiation of the sun. The Gau Seva Ayog claims that a house painted with cow dung could be the most potent form of protection against radiation thanks to its powerful anti-radiation qualities.

UP's minister for animal husbandry, Laxmi Kant Bajpai, says the department is seeking scientific verification of the claims. Developed by the Kanpur Goshala Society at Panki, samples of the cow dung-based distemper are being sent to the Bhabha Atomic Research Centre for the required tests.

According to Bajpai: "There is enough traditional evidence to support the theory, but we are looking for scientific clearance of these claims."

The Kanpur Goshala Society has developed the distemper in five earthly colours. Tiles using cow dung as base have also been developed by the Society. The Society's general secretary said that once the scientific validation comes through, they would be stepping up production capacity, which is currently limited.

60% Patients Consult Chemists, Not Doctors

People don't take their health seriously enough, as this survey indicates. A consumer group, VOICE (Voluntary Organisation in Interest of Consumer Education), conducted a study that discovered 60 per cent of patients consult chemists to decide which medicines they should take, instead of consulting a doctor.

After conducting a study in UP and Karnataka, VOICE has voiced fears that this could lead to unsafe medical practices. The group said it was disconcerting that only 40 per cent of patients visited doctors.

The study also uncovered the extent of the menace of spurious drugs. Up to 43 per cent of doctors claimed they had noticed fake drugs being sold in the market, although just seven per cent of patients said they were aware of such drugs. When the drugs weren't spurious, there were other problems. For instance, the drugs weren't being stored properly. In UP, the study found that over 30 per cent of chemists did not use refrigerators and life-saving drugs and injectables were simply being kept on the shelves.

The National Pharmaceutical Pricing Authority, a government body meant to control the prices of drugs in the country, sponsored the study.

Physicians Susceptible to Depression and Suicide

'Tis truly said, 'Physician, heal thyself.' That's easier said than done, going by a report that doctors worldwide are twice as likely to fall prey to depression and suicide than the patients they treat.

This startling finding was made public at a seminar held in Delhi in the last quarter of 2002. It explains why the Indian Medical Association has laid the rule that doctors must undergo a medical check-up every year. The doctors' susceptibility to these ailments is due to their erratic work hours and hectic profession and lifestyle. Besides, doctors know either too much or too little about their own health problems.

Delhi psychiatrist Sanjay Chugh also makes the surprising revelation that each day at least one of the patients who consult him is a doctor with depression. He adds that the incidence of suicide is the highest amongst psychiatrists.

A senior gastro-enterologist at the Indraprastha Apollo Hospital also reveals that doctors often take medication without being aware of the composition and side effects.

India has Record 17,000 Pharma Manufacturers

Dr K Weerasuriya, an expert with the World Health Organisation, says that India is perhaps the only country where a large number of drug formulations and combinations are promoted. "As many as 60,000 formulations of medicines are in circulation in India, many of which are costly, hazardous and irrational drugs," he said.

While Britain has less than 400 pharmaceutical manufacturers, India has a whopping 17,000! Thanks to this, aggressive marketing is not uncommon and it includes corrupt practices and huge incentives.

The next time you are prescribed antibiotics for treating an ordinary cough and cold, remember that this is unsound advice and a total waste of your money. The long-term side effects could be that you end up developing antibiotic resistance.

Hospital Offers Three Lines of Treatment

You have heard of allopathic, ayurvedic and homeopathic hospitals. Maybe even unani hospitals. But have you heard of a hospital that offers allopathy, homeopathy and ayurveda treatments?

Dr Hegdewar Hospital in east Delhi is India's first government-run hospital that gives patients a choice between these three medical disciplines. And patients should be happy as ever about this, but that isn't exactly the case. Choosing between the three, apparently, is far from easy. Many patients end up shuttling between the different wings and disciplines before finding the right doctor.

In many cases, it is the registration clerk who makes the choice for confused patients. In case the patient is still clueless about which doctor to see, he is referred to the allopathic doctor.

Medical superintendent Dr P Raju revealed: "We get 350 patients every day. Of them, a few new patients are not able to choose a treatment system. Such patients are sent to the medical OPD and then, depending on the urgency of the situation, are referred to other systems... Our hospital has introduced a new concept and there are bound to be teething troubles. We have clearly instructed all our doctors to set aside their egos and refer patients to other wings without any hesitation."

That's means, if a homeopath finds that a patient is not improving, he will then refer the patient to another system.

The hospital has also set aside 10 beds for each system for surgeries, since surgical interventions are also done by homeopaths and ayurvedic doctors. The hospital currently has 200 beds.

Wallet-reducing Techniques to Sleep

Is insomnia your bugbear? Do not worry, there are new - and expensive - ways to ensure you sleep better! Sleep labs, for instance.

Doctors say that how one sleeps determines how healthy one is. Insomnia and excessive daytime drowsiness are said to be some of the over 200 sleep-related disorders.

Delhi's Sir Ganga Ram Hospital, All-India Institute of Medical Sciences, Apollo Hospital and Batra Hospital are some of the many places that have opened 'sleep labs' where a person can sleep overnight, while body functions are carefully monitored. Thereafter, doctors study the reports to zero in on the problem.

While the night stay will cost only around Rs.1,500–2,000, the actual therapy costs much more and is not being openly publicised for obvious reasons - so that you do not lose sleep over the cost!

Hospitality & Tourism

Chhattisgarh's Pure Magic

One of India's new states, carved out of UP in November 2000, Chhattisgarh has some unique features that should make it a tourist's delight, if promoted in the right way.

Dr A Jayathilak, MD, Chhattisgarh Tourism Board, reveals that the state has the densest forest cover second only to the Amazon, with forests covering an incredible 46 per cent of the state. India's biggest waterfall is located at Chitrakote, half an hour's drive from Jagdalpur, headquarters of Bastar district.

Furthermore, Chhattisgarh is the only place in India where the soil is still not exposed to pesticides and one can get truly organic food. Believe it or not, there are more than 22,000 varieties of rice grown here.

Finally, Chhattisgarh is one of India's few power-surplus states. And the best part for road-bound tourists: one can drive from Raipur to Bastar – a distance of 300 km – in less than five hours, which is a miracle in India!

How the Taj was Born

On 17 December 2003 the Taj Mahal Hotel turned 100. There are some strange but true facts connected with the Hotel's history. The idea for this Indian five-star hotel first came into Sir Jamshedji Tata's mind over a century ago, when he was prevented from entering the Majestic Hotel (then Bombay's best address for tourists), thanks to its Whites Only policy in the days of the Raj. A furious Jamshedji vowed he would build a hotel so classy that people wouldn't give the Majestic Hotel a second look. And so it came to pass...

In the early years, the Taj supposedly had a sign that read 'No Dogs and South Africans Allowed'. Dogs were barred for obvious reasons. And South Africans were presumably being given their due for Apartheid.

Another incredible fact is that the profits from the Hotel go to charity.

Taj and the Raj Syndrome

Strangely, over a century after Jamshedji Tata's humiliation through being barred entry from a hotel premises, the Taj Bengal earned the dubious distinction of indulging in a similar practice. Eighteen students from West Bengal who had won scholarships were denied permission to enter the Taj Bengal from the front entrance since they were wearing chappals. Instead, they were asked to enter the premises from the rear entrance.

The students had gone to a function being held at the Taj Bengal to collect their scholarships. The function was organised by the Moni Bhowmick Educational Foundation and was graced by the West Bengal Chief Minister. Some of the impoverished students were tribals who had made the grade by studying under lanterns in a room shared by family and livestock. All the students had scored over 80 per cent in the higher secondary exams. Some had secured admission into the Calcutta Medical College and the Jadavpur University engineering course.

Moni Bhowmick, the scholarship founder, consoled the students saying that he was confident that many of them would re-enter the Hotel from the front door. Bhowmick himself hailed from a poor Tamluck family. Overcoming adverse circumstances, he is now an affluent physicist in Los Angeles.

Perhaps the Taj management could institute a via media to ensure such Raj-mentality discrimination is no longer practised, considering what its own founder faced. Ironically, while Indian hotels still practise this discrimination, hotels in the West can be sued if they do not allow non-shoed people to enter. Wonder what the Taj would do if barefooted MF Husain paid a visit!

Mandatory Visit to Monuments for Delhi Schoolchildren

Thanks to the aftermath of 9/11, if foreign tourists won't come to India, never mind. The Delhi Government has devised ways to drag Indians to tourist spots – and so what if they happen to be schoolchildren! The *Dilli sarkar* has made it compulsory for Delhi's schoolchildren to visit city monuments at least once a year. Delhi education minister Rajkumar Chauhan claims the move is not just an attempt to "popularise monuments, but also has educative value".

As of January 2003, it is mandatory for the 1,109 government-run schools in Delhi to organise trips to monuments. The government proposes to extend the directive to public schools "shortly".

By the way, in Delhi 'public schools' are actually privately-run schools - unlike in a city like Mumbai, where a 'public school' would refer to a municipal school run by the government. While in Mumbai, well-heeled parents look down upon and avoid 'public schools', in Delhi rich parents always opt for public schools!

Delhi Tourism and Transport Development Corporation MD Rajiv Talwar says they will "provide bus services and meals to school kids at concessional rates, apart from tourist guides and literature on monuments".

If things work out as planned, Delhi's school kids will be more environmentally conscious, while the city's heritage monuments will also see the moolah coming in to ensure better upkeep.

Human Affairs

Sikh Wins the World's Funniest Joke Contest

Don't believe people who tell you that Indians lack a sense of humour. Why, we have people who can not only tell the best jokes, but also do so at their own expense, like Jaspal Bhatti. Small wonder then that in October 2002 it was a Sikh who won a contest for narrating the world's funniest joke.

Gurpal Gossal is a 31-year-old second generation Indian immigrant from Manchester whose joke beat 40,000 other entries from over 70 countries. The world's funniest joke goes thus...

Two shikaris are out hunting in the jungles when one of them collapses in a heap. His eyes are glazed and he doesn't seem to be breathing. Frantic, the other shikari draws his cellphone and calls an emergency service. "Help! My friend is dead! What should I do?"

Responds the operator: "Calm down. Calm down. We can handle this. But first you have to make sure he's dead."

There is momentary silence and then a rifle shot shatters the calm jungle air. The guy is back on the line: "Okay! Now what?"

The joke contest concluded a 13-month-long scientific experiment launched in Britain by Dr Richard Wiseman, a psychologist who was seeking to delve "into the psychology of humour". The study was conducted on the Internet's "laugh-lab" and invited entries that were given worldwide ratings on a five-point Giggleometer. Two million ratings poured in. The experiment is also said to have identified the brain's laughter centre – a region near the back of the frontal lobes.

The Largest Joint Family

Most modern couples prefer to go nuclear, under the pretext of enjoying "privacy", disregarding the benefits of the traditional Indian joint family. But Aranmanai in Theni, Tamil Nadu, is a shining example of the benefits of the joint family system. Aranmanai (the Tamil word for *palace*) is a white and blue building that every villager on the Theni-Periyakulam road knows - thanks to its 127 occupants, who form the largest joint family in Tamil Nadu!

A visit to the household during the day strikes you with its sheer... silence! With the children at schools or in the fields and most of the men and women also in the fields (tending 300 acres), one finds only a handful of ladies at home to take care of the daily chores.

For the record, the family comprises 40 brothers and 20 sisters, which includes first cousins. There are 20 couples and 21 children. For over four generations, the family has been together. About 50 direct descendants live elsewhere in Tamil Nadu. Ettamuthu Naicker is the eldest at 72, while two one-year-old grandsons are the youngest.

Aranmanai comprises two huge yards. The larger one is enclosed by a low-roof structure with 24 rooms, two kitchens, a prayer hall and one television. Every month, two different women cook the joint family's food, but each family can eat the food privately in their rooms.

V. Ramaraj manages the family, since he was elected the "family manager" by other relatives a few years ago. Every family member performs the tasks allocated to him or her. Says 20-year-old N Jeyapadi: "Unless everyone performs their task it would be difficult to run such a large family."

South Gujarat Addicts Hooked to Scorpion Stings

When it comes to getting their high, drug addicts will go to any lengths, like sniffing glue, taking cough syrups or other dangerous substances as a substitute. But elite addicts in south Gujarat have another deadly means of getting their high - scorpion stings!

On weekdays at locations across the tribal areas of Bharuch district, sting merchants move between Walia to Dediapada, setting up stalls under a tree. Expensive cars stop by and the young addicts get their sting for rates ranging between Rs.150 and Rs.200 per shot. The addicts - from surrounding areas like Bharuch, Vadodara and Surat - have been visiting the sting merchants regularly for the past two years.

Says sting merchant Nathu: "You won't die... try it once... it's a lifetime's experience." He then produces an aluminium container with a perforated lid from his bag and gingerly strokes an agitated brown scorpion. The six-legged creature crawls up a client's fingers, lifts its tail and strikes, injecting venom into the man's bloodstream that gives an illusory sensation of floating and momentary pain.

Clients are charged before they are given a sting. The sting merchants confine their activities between Walia and Dediapada, a 40-km stretch where there is an abundance of scorpions. Though these scorpions are poisonous, the venom is not enough to kill humans. Which is why the trade continues...

Gujarat Electoral Candidate Begs for Deposit Money

The December 2002 elections in Gujarat had some unusual contestants. One of them who stood out was Prahlad Solanki, a manhole worker who was given the boot a year ago. With dreams of making it to the State Assembly, Solanki decided to throw his hat into the electoral fray. Except for a minor problem - the stipulated deposit of Rs.2,500.

Undaunted, the man came up with just the right solution. While other candidates went around seeking votes, Solanki went from door to door, bowl in hand, seeking donations in Sherkotda constituency. And he was willing to accept any sum in rupees or paisa - 50, 25 or even 10 paise was welcome.

Just four days after hitting the dirt road, Solanki had Rs.2,500 in the kitty... and Rs.500 to spare! The next stop was the electoral office with two boxes of loose change. The sight of the deposit being deposited in *chiller* had the returning officer stumped. The electoral officers initially refused to accept the deposit in coins. But Solanki told them he was unemployed and this was the only way he could cough up the deposit amount. When the electoral officers did consent to accepting the loose change, it took them over two hours to count the dough, according to the amused Solanki.

After the elections, one hasn't heard any more of Prahlad Solanki. Perhaps he's still counting the balance *chiller*!

One Nostril at a Time, Please

Did you know that humans breathe only from one nostril at a time? Indian yogis have known this fact for the past few millennia, thanks to yogic techniques of breath control.

Modern research now confirms that at any given time only one of the nostrils functions, with each nostril switching their olfactory roles several times a day. Furthermore, each nostril is said to smell the surroundings differently. Ever since man began living in urban settings, though, his sense of smell has been taking a beating, with olfactory acuity said to diminish after the age of 35.

Annual Ghost *Mela* in MP Village

You may have heard of *melas* (fairs) of different kinds, including animal melas, but ever heard of a ghost mela? Strange but true, there is indeed a mela for ghosts and evil spirits - not to entertain, but to exorcise the *bhoot-prets*.

Every year beginning on *Paush Purnima* day and ending on *Basant Panchami*, Malajpur village in southern Madhya Pradesh holds a *Bhoot-Pret ka Mela*. In 2003, the fair began on 17 January and concluded on 6 February. This year, about 5,000 "possessed" persons from MP, Rajasthan, Maharashtra and Andhra Pradesh were brought to Guru Deoji Sant Mandir at Malajpur, 290 km south of Bhopal. On *Paush Purnima* day, over 65,000 visitors visited the village, which included families of past and present victims. The attendance on the concluding day was reportedly around 100,000.

A typical scene involves the temple priest sprinkling holy water on a "possessed" woman and shouting at her, inquiring "Who are you?", as the victim shrieks and shakes with hair dishevelled and eyes seemingly popping out of their sockets.

The head priest Chandra Singh Mahant reveals that the fair is being held annually for the past 250 years. Mahant claims that two banyan trees in the temple compound have "several lakh ghosts, who have been expelled from human bodies". The temple is the *samadhi* of Guru Deoji Sant, a Rajput from Rajasthan whose family is supposed to have settled in Malajpur. Born around AD 1700, Deoji Sant revealed supernatural powers and performed miracles from an early age.

The legend goes that Deoji had told the villagers to bury him in a *samadhi* and exhume his body after 11 months. The villagers made the mistake of digging his resting place nine months later. What they found was the foetus of an unborn child. They buried it again. The tradition of exorcising evil spirits at his *samadhi* slowly became a ritual and the fair is held ever since.

Thanks to this ghostly tradition, Malajpur village boasts of about 200 priests, who are supposedly trained in the "art of expelling evil spirits".

Childbirth in an Incredible Location

You have heard of women giving birth in trains, aircraft and water. However, these cases were either inadvertent or deliberate. But have you ever heard of women giving birth in trees? Believe it or not, that's exactly what the fear of elephants is forcing women in Dumka district of Jharkhand to do.

At the onset of labour pains, women in Dumka climb up trees (how pregnant women manage this feat is a miracle in itself!) to avoid "rogue" elephants that have killed quite a few people. In May 2003, Duli Maharani of Jora Aam village gave birth to her child perched on a mango tree. Urmila Devi of Dumka also delivered her child up a tree.

To avoid dangerous elephants and facilitate smooth delivery, the adivasis have now begun constructing machans for their pregnant women.

The Right to Die

Believe it or not, some senior citizens in Kerala are petitioning the courts for permission to end their lives. While euthanasia or mercy killing by a medical practitioner for those suffering from incurable diseases is heard of in the West, in India this was not an issue until recently...

In October 2002, a petition filed in the Kerala High Court was dismissed. A retired teacher of Trissur, CA Thomas filed the petition in 1996. In his seventies, Thomas made a fervent plea that he be granted legal sanction to end his life. Although a Christian, Thomas quoted Hindu Scriptures and ancient Indian systems, pointing out how such a system would be useful to individuals and society at large.

It was pointed out that a person could donate his wealth and healthy organs when s/he decides to die of his or her own volition. The person could then seek medical help to pass away peacefully at a ripe age. The concept is said to have existed in ancient times, through the Hindu ritual of a person selecting *vanprasth* and living in seclusion the way he liked in the last days of his life.

The High Court dismissed Thomas' petition as untenable.

Another petition filed at the sub-court in Ernakulam remains undecided since the government has failed to respond in any manner. A wealthy industrialist, Kochauseph Chittilappilly, filed this second petition in 1998, stating that what he sought was legal sanction, not mercy killing. Chittilappilly (47 years old when he filed the petition) had stated that he considered 70 years a fairly good cut-off age for one to contemplate death.

Although the sub-court had asked the state to respond, for the past four years there has been no response. A successful industrialist from Kochi, Chittilappilly feels it should be the right of an individual to decide when to quit living.

The Rickshaw-puller Who Distributes Blankets

We have heard countless stories of charity and philanthropy, where the rich and the super-rich give and it simply doesn't hurt them. But stories where people give when it hurts are rare.

One such true story comes from Lucknow, in the form of 36-year-old rickshaw-puller Mohammad Ahmad. During the chilling winter evenings of January 2003, Ahmad was seen distributing blankets to beggars. Ahmad is a rickshaw-puller during the day and a security guard at night. So obviously he makes just enough to eke out his living. But whatever little he does manage to save from his extra labour, he sets aside a part of it to buy blankets.

His story of what inspired him tells some more about the selfless man. "A few years ago, I saw a man sitting in a car distributing blankets on a winter night. He apparently finished with his stock when an old beggar managed to steer through the crowd, begging for a blanket," recalls Ahmad.

The very next morning, Ahmad had bought a blanket, traced the old beggar and handed over the blanket, which could have been the difference between life and death for the latter. The tears in the old beggar's eyes and the blessings that he mumbled gave Ahmad a new purpose in life.

Will every reader promise to buy a few blankets and distribute these every winter amongst the poor? It will cost you just a few hundred rupees, but will save precious lives.

Peeping Tom Landlord Lands in Trouble

Dirty landlords have their own bag of tricks. But 35-year-old Pankaj Chopra of Delhi's South Patel Nagar ensured he had more than an eyeful. In fact, this voyeuristic landlord was enjoying his peep show with not one but five female tenants.

Chopra had a web camera installed in the first floor bathroom, which the five young women shared amongst themselves. In the age group of 24 to 30, the women had moved into the Chopra household in June 2002. While the Chopra family lived on the ground floor, the tenants lived on the first floor. Pankaj Chopra had built a room on the second floor, above the tenants' room, which he used as his office. Naturally, he had a computer installed in the office. The web camera in the first floor bathroom was connected to the computer by a cable, through which Chopra was able to watch the women on his computer and download all the nude images.

Chopra enjoyed nearly seven months of voyeuristic delights. In the fourth week of December, one of the women was having a bath on a Sunday when she spotted the camera.

The aghast women complained to the Patel Nagar police post-haste. Chopra's house was raided and the computer seized. The nude pictures were also confiscated by the cops, which Chopra had downloaded onto floppies.

The next time you move into a rented accommodation that you are sharing with the landlord, don't forget to snoop around for snoopy cameras!

Language Talk

The Bastardisation of English

Hinglish in India perhaps first made its appearance in print when the saucy Shobha De was editing the film glossy *Stardust* in the early 70s. Another *Stardust* editor Uma Rao also played her part in giving Hinglish currency. Then came the television boom in the 90s, which saw newscasters from Zee TV and Star give further mileage to Hinglish.

Although purists may be turning in their graves at this bastardisation of the Queen's English, the new millennium has seen more vigorous churning, thanks to the advent of Internet chats and mobile SMS. Written English is quickly being reduced to "half-baked jargon". The new words include *chilax* (chill + relax), *dopsy* (a person who is spaced out), *baldie* (for a Rs.500 note, since it features the Father of the Nation), *chape* (someone who hangs around like a leech), and *phataka* (a sexy girl).

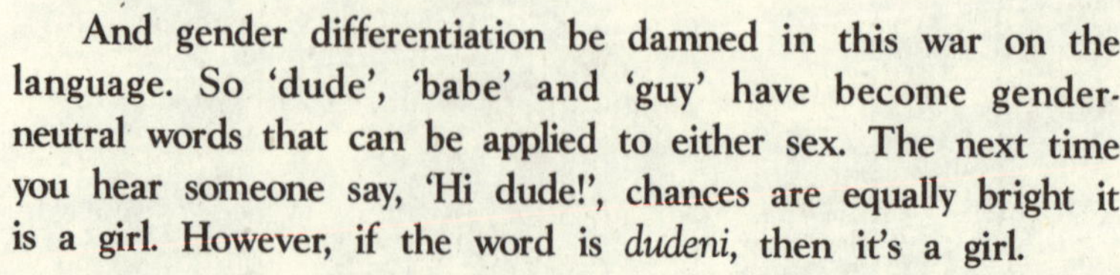

And gender differentiation be damned in this war on the language. So 'dude', 'babe' and 'guy' have become gender-neutral words that can be applied to either sex. The next time you hear someone say, 'Hi dude!', chances are equally bright it is a girl. However, if the word is *dudeni*, then it's a girl.

Anjana Sharma, head of department, English Literature, Lady Shriram College, Delhi, opines that most students don't read anymore and only end up learning the contemporary colloquial English. Besides, speaking correct English, feels Sharma, is no longer considered "cool".

An MBA student blames the Americanisation of English for this, with words like 'wanna', 'gonna' and 'kinda' now becoming legal tender. So today's teens greet each other with 'Whassup'; mean Yes when they say 'yeah', 'yo', 'yup' or 'yope'; fill their cars with 'gas' instead of petrol and snigger if you ask for a 'rubber' instead of an 'eraser'. While 'rubber' meant 'eraser' 20 years ago, it now means 'condom'!

Some Languages, Dialects and Scripts Going into Limbo

The world supposedly has some 5,000 languages and dialects. Of this number, India itself reportedly boasts of over 1,600 languages and dialects! Yet, many languages like Sanskrit are almost in limbo. And fewer and fewer Sindhis now speak their own language, Sindhi.

Another tragedy in the making will be the demise of Sharda, the script of Kashmir. Indeed, Kashmir was once known as Sharda Desha. Today, few Kashmiris understand the script. Worse, some temple priests in Kashmir haven't even heard of Sharda!

Professor TN Kunju, one of the last Sharda scholars in Srinagar, can no longer keep pace with the documentation required – for instance, the cataloguing of 300 books. And the last man who could read the script in the Srinagar University library reportedly retired 30 years ago. Prof. Kunju bemoans the fact that most of the rare books could be found in the libraries of Kashmiri Pandits. When they fled the state, they left their priceless books behind, which were later sold by the kilo.

Sharda was used in Kashmir since AD 9th century, having evolved directly from Brahmi. This is the script that the Kashmiri language was written in. Just three decades ago, horoscopes and birth records were written in Sharda! Sadly, youngsters now write Kashmiri in the Urdu and Devnagri scripts. Prof. Kunju reveals that his mother kept her household accounts in Sharda. "Today, how will students of Sharda find a job?" Kunju muses.

Love & Sex

Condom Bike Spreads the Safe Sex Message

Condoms are one of the best methods to spread the message of safe sex. A citizen of Hyderabad has, however, come up with a "faster" way of spreading the message - a motorbike shaped like a condom!

K Sudhakar, a car designer, says he intends spreading the message about the virtues of condom usage by going across the country on his personally designed bike. The unique condom motorbike was launched at a club in Hyderabad in end November 2002. It is equipped with a tape recorder that plays messages on the virtues of using condoms, including the prevention of the deadly AIDS. The message also educates people on how AIDS is contracted.

With a 60-cc engine, the bike seats just one person and is made of light steel. It is equipped with a headlight, tail lamps and indicators and also has a flap that slides over the handle when the bike is not in use. The driver simply presses a remote control button to push back the flap. The tape begins playing the moment the flap covers the handle.

It's not AIDS messages only that the tape plays. It also tells listeners about the discovery of the condom: "In 3000 BC, King Minos of Crete used a fish bladder to protect himself from the risks of unprotected sex." There are more condom facts. The first mass production of condoms was in 1844 by Goodyear and Hancock. The first condom ad (Dr Power's French Preventives) appeared in *The New York Times*. The era of the Pill and the sexual revolution of the 1960s almost put paid to condom usage... Until AIDS officially burst onto the scene in 1981!

Incidentally, Sudhakar has designed cars in the shape of brinjals and onions! This time around, he wanted to do something more worthwhile and thus was born the condom bike. With Andhra Pradesh ranking number two in AIDS cases, the designer felt this was one way in which he could contribute to the cause of arresting the killer disease.

Media Wars

TV Channels Boosting Newspaper Readership!

The slow death of the print media had been foretold after the advent of cable and satellite television. The findings of the Delhi-based Centre for Media Studies (CMS) are a revelation in the opposite direction, however.

An ongoing study by CMS reveals that newspapers are the unexpected winners in the TV channel proliferation war currently on. TV news hasn't adversely affected newspaper readership habits, but left readers asking for more news - which is obviously provided by newspapers. Indeed, what's happening is that the more news viewers watch on TV, the greater their tendency to pick up a newspaper and reconfirm the news, according to the CMS study titled, *Appetiser effect of TV news on newspaper readership*.

Says N Bhaskara Rao, chairman of CMS: "TV news is adding to the readership as well as credibility of mainline daily newspapers."

The study was based on a survey of 150 viewer-readers conducted for over a year in New Delhi, Chennai, Kolkata and Hyderabad. The study discovered that the respondents who watched TV news the previous night spent 60 per cent more time reading newspapers the next morning. They did this seeking more details and to reconfirm the credibility of the TV news. In fact, the survey found that the credibility of mainline newspapers had improved over the past one year compared to TV news.

CMS predicts this "complementary phenomenon" between the two media will grow over the years.

Nature

Killing Peacocks an Offence, Possession of Feathers, Not

During a discussion on the Wildlife (Protection) and Amendment Bill (which came up for discussion in the Lok Sabha in mid-December 2002), Minister for Environment TR Baalu said the purpose of the Bill was to make wildlife laws more stringent. Maneka Gandhi also spoke about the ironical situation of India's national bird, the peacock.

While the killing of peacocks was a cognisable offence, the sale or possession of peacock feathers was not! Unless a ban was imposed forthwith on the sale of peacock feathers, the national bird would go the way of the dodo. With poachers indulging in mass poisoning of the birds, they were being killed in increasing numbers all over the country. The birds did not shed the feathers available in the market naturally, as some apologists try to make out, but obtained these after killing them, Maneka insisted.

Power Modes

Horsepower Will Now be Bull-power

Stephenson may have used steam power to fuel his engine. But in these days of rising costs, who has the time for all that complicated bull. We Indians prefer to keep things simple, environment-friendly and cheap. Thinking along these lines, the Kanpur Gau Shala Society, Panki branch, has come up with an incredible innovation that was first used by a Varanasi farmer. With IIT engineers from Kanpur and Delhi said to be giving it the final touches, the innovation will then be offered for sale.

An amalgam of ancient and modern expertise, the technique comprises a pair of bullocks moving in a circle around an axis. The centre has a fixed rotor that moves at high speeds of up to 1,500 revolutions per minute. This rustic contraption is said to generate up to 2 kilowatt of electricity. IIT engineers are presently working on technical improvements and standardisation to increase the production up to 4 KW. If the idea works out in practice, diesel generator makers will be wiped out of the UP markets in the coming years.

The Gau Shala plans large-scale production of the innovation with two objectives in mind: saving bulls from the abattoir and helping the power-starved state of Uttar Pradesh. According to the manager of the Panki unit, Purushottam Toshniwal, one bull-powered generator could light up to 60 homes. And an improved version could have much better results. With most villagers already being bull owners, what's required is only that they buy the accessories for the bull-generator, which is not a very costly affair.

Best of all, the contraption also comes with a gearbox! This is to ensure that the speed of the generator is regulated so as not to tire out the animals quickly. The electricity that is thereby produced is stored in a condenser. It can then be used when required.

...If Not, There's Solar Power

For those who feel bull-power may be pure bull, solar energy could be a viable option. In fact, solar power could light up as many as 80,000 villages in India. A spokesperson for the Ministry of Non-conventional Energy Sources (MNES) said India is a "sun-drenched" country, receiving four to seven kilowatt per hour energy from the sun in every square metre, on average.

To tap this cheap and permanent energy source, rooftops can be fitted with photovoltaic solar (PVS) modules. The modules can be charged with solar energy during the day, which will directly convert this into electricity that will be stored in a battery. This electricity can then be consumed in the night.

For starters, one needs only to invest in the installation of the modules, said an officer of the MNES, at the India International Trade Fair, held at Pragati Maidan, Delhi, in the last quarter of 2002. To cover 500 square yards, the cost for a PVS module works out to Rs.25,000. Although the start-up cost is high, one can break even in the first year itself, through the savings on the monthly electricity bills that one would otherwise have to pay.

Since India receives 5,000 trillion kilo watt per hour of sun annually, this is more than enough to meet the nation's total annual energy requirement. Are the powers-that-be reading this?

Science & Technology

Life Came from Thin Air

How did life begin on earth? This is a scientific enigma that the best brains have been trying to solve for years. Astrophysicists Jayant Narlikar and Chandra Wickremasinghe claim that life materialised out of thin air. No, that's not meant to be a joke.

The Indian-Sri Lankan duo examined air samples collected some 41 kilometres away from the earth. In January 2002, with the aid of an indigenously made cryogenic sampler set afloat high above the earth's stratosphere, ISRO (Indian Space Research Organisation) scientists conducted this operation from Hyderabad.

Incidentally, it was Fred Hoyle and Wickremasinghe who put forward the panspermia theory that comets could have been the carriers that delivered extraterrestrial micro-organisms in a frozen state to earth.

In a Press Conference at the Inter-University Centre for Astronomy and Astrophysics, Pune in October 2002, Narlikar revealed that the cryo-sampler experiment conducted in collaboration with ISRO was a fall-out of this theory. Through a balloon, the cyro-sampler with 16 sterilised probes was sent some 41 km into the stratosphere from the TIFR (Tata Institute of Fundamental Research) balloon facility at Hyderabad.

The probes collected air samples from four different heights, which were then filtered and later tested at laboratories. Some bacteria were detected in the air samples, which were not common contaminants. Nor had these been used before in the labs where the tests were conducted. And no such growth was found on control membranes that were not exposed to the air samples.

Since these micro-organisms were alien to earth, it could only mean that "extraterrestrial life" had perhaps been intercepted. But scientists are not uncorking the champagne until confirmatory tests come up with conclusive proof substantiating the panspermia theory.

If substantiated, besides proving that we are indeed progeny of extraterrestrials as claimed by writers like Erich Von Daniken, it will also mean that life in the universe has much more in common than we currently comprehend.

SMS a Lifeline for the Hearing Impaired

We all know that SMS (short message service) is especially popular amongst the younger generation, for obvious and not-so-obvious reasons. Yet, there is an unknown segment that already finds SMS an indispensable part of their lives - the hearing impaired.

For those with a hearing handicap, SMS is a lifeline. The SMS traffic amongst the hearing impaired is said to be "massive". Most of them send around 50 messages a day, some much more! Even those who are not so well off spend a significant amount of their pay packets on SMS.

According to Arun Rao, executive director of Deaf Way (an NGO working for empowerment of the deaf): "These people are not earning huge salaries. Yet they spend quite a bit on SMS-ing because for them it is a lifeline. A mobile phone has become the most coveted possession, the favourite birthday gift for a deaf person."

Prior to the SMS era, something as simple as rescheduling a meeting was a nightmare. And the situation was worse for those who were totally deaf. AS Narayanan, who works in the Ministry of Industries, reveals that earlier he would be worried like hell if he was late for a meeting. This meant finding a "hearing person", communicating that he wanted to make a call and then having that person pass on the message to another "hearing person", who in turn would have to convey the message for him. Naturally, this was a cumbersome process, with no certainty that the message would be conveyed or conveyed correctly. Now, all Narayanan has to do is send an SMS.

Plastic Roads May be Round the Corner

With plastic being a non-biodegradable substance, its disposal is a major nuisance, with burning also not a healthy solution, thanks to the toxic fumes it gives out. But Professor R Vasudevan of Thiagaraja Engineering College in Madurai may have discovered the perfect solution to this vexing problem.

Hot bitumen mixed with molten plastic waste could be the perfect solution, while also helping improve our battered roads. The professor of chemistry from Tamil Nadu has even found official favour, with the Chennai Municipal Corporation agreeing to test his formula.

In the words of Prof. Vasudevan: "It's a simple procedure where plastic waste is mixed with hot bitumen before it is laid. Since plastic waste like cups, carry bags etc are heated only up to 170 degrees centigrade, they form a molten paste and get mixed with bitumen. Since the waste is not incinerated, no toxic gases are released. As only non-chloride polymer waste is used, the question of chlorine seepage is also avoided."

The plastic increases the road's load-bearing capacity, makes it more heat resistant and prevents rainwater from seeping down.

Delhi Researchers Develop Thorn-less Roses

According to Delhi development minister Haroon Yusuf, researchers at the Indian Agriculture Research Institute, Pusa, have developed a number of high-tech crops, including orange-coloured capsicum, seedless cucumber and rose plants without thorns.

Says Yusuf: "Keeping Delhi's weather in mind, these crops have been specifically developed to offer higher yield and better quality." The thorn-less roses have been named Mohit and are pink in colour.

Strange Tales

The Origins of Hindi Cinema

In 1911, when Dadasaheb Phalke - the Father of Indian Cinema - decided to enter filmmaking, he did not have enough funds. So he sold his wife's jewellery and made the trick film, *Birth of a Pea Plant*, which was shot one frame a day to show the plant growing. Phalke showed this film to Yashwant Nadkarni, a dealer in photographic equipment, who was so amazed by the film that he agreed to back Phalke financially. With this funding, Phalke established the Phalke Film Company. In 1913, he made Hindi cinema's first film, *Raja Harishchandra*.

Why Gandhi Wore Only Khadi

After his arrival from South Africa, Mahatma Gandhi was once passing through a village, along with his wife Kasturba. Gandhi noticed an elderly woman sitting outside her hut, wearing a dirty saree. Gandhi told Kasturba to ask the lady why she could not clean her clothes. Gandhi opined that while it was not a crime to be poor, cleanliness was essential.

Kasturba walked up to the lady and engaged her in conversation. It transpired that she had only one set of clothes! The lady queried that if she cleaned that one, what would she wear?

Her response and her abject poverty disturbed Gandhi. That very day Gandhi decided to sacrifice all clothes and wear only a loincloth. He vowed that until every Indian had proper clothing, he would spend his life in a loincloth.

The Blind Man Who Conquered Everest

Helen Keller didn't let her blindness handicap her. In the twenty-first century, Eric Weihenmayer has proved to be another role model for the blind. On 25 May 2001, Eric Weihenmayer became the first blind man in history to reach the summit of the world's highest peak - Mount Everest.

Eric lost his vision when he was 13, but he never let his blindness submerge his passion for mountaineering. Eric is also the author of *Touch the Top of the World,* which tells the story of his conquest of the highest peaks in the world.

Innovator Makes Teeth, Cycles and Hand Pumps from Bamboo

Dodhi Pathak, a folk singer from Nalbari in Assam, won the first national innovation award for making low-cost bamboo teeth dentures. Dodhi Pathak chisels cheap bamboo teeth for villagers in the Nalabari district, since they cannot afford the costly treatment of regular dentists. The National Innovation Foundation, set up by the department of science and technology, annually awards people who solve technological problems in cost-effective and innovative ways. Pathak's teeth have now been registered and possibilities of commercial production are being explored.

In his late forties, this singer turned to bamboo when he lost all his front teeth in an accident in 1994. As he could not afford the false teeth available with the dentist, he used underground nodes of bamboo to make his own. Pathak says he can chew easily and even bite into meat with ease. The frontal incisors cost him Rs.30 and the molars Rs.50. The teeth can be fixed permanently or made into dentures. Pathak takes just 30 minutes to make a tooth. To ensure pearly white teeth, Pathak coats the brown bamboo dentures with melted plastic from toothbrushes.

This innovator hasn't stopped at bamboo teeth. When he couldn't afford even a second-hand bicycle, he decided to construct one himself from locally available material – the ubiquitous bamboo! All the parts of his bicycle are made from bamboo, except the tyres and tubes.

He has also developed a working model of a hand pump made from... what else but bamboo! Suitable for lifting both underground water and pond water, even the piston, valve, barrel, handle and all other parts of the pump have been fashioned from bamboo.

India's Self-proclaimed Witch

Remember all the stories about witches you heard as a child, but knew such people didn't exist today? Well, you are dead wrong! Meet Ipsita Roy Chakraverti, India's self-proclaimed modern-day witch. Ipsita lives in New Delhi's Railway Colony, since her husband Joyanta Das is a senior officer in Northern Railway.

What makes Ipsita stand apart is her knowledge of Wicca or witchcraft. In fact, Ipsita has used her knowledge of witchcraft to help people overcome their problems. Ipsita says Wicca is not a profession for her: "It is a way of life to make you (especially women) strong to cope with life... I do try my best to help people in distress by passing on 'some energy'." She admits she does not know where the energy comes from. "But it helps the person to come out of the situation."

Her success can be measured by the fact that she has written books on the subject. HarperCollins published her autobiography, *Beloved Witch*, in 2000. Her second book, *Sacred Evil* – a collection of short stories based on her encounters with the unknown – was released in May 2003. After the release of her first book, she was invited to various august forums (such as

IIT and the Confederation of Indian Industries) for lectures and discussions.

Currently, Ipsita is working on her third book, tentatively titled *Every Strong Woman is a Witch*, where she plans to reveal her secrets about witchcraft. Ipsita also runs an NGO, National Youth Brigade, based in Hooghly, which works with women and children. The NGO was funded from the royalties she received from her first book. If only India had many more witches like Ipsita!

The Saga of the Mahars

Strange as it may seem, the British didn't conquer India with troops of white soldiers fighting Indians – they conquered India with armies composed mostly of Indians!

For instance, consider the 1818 Battle of Koregaon – the last Anglo-Maratha battle that helped conclusively establish British rule in western India and completed the East India Company's territorial conquest of the country. Here, it was the Mahars (an 'untouchable' community of Maharashtra) in the British army who helped defeat the Marathas! The British force in this battle comprised barely 774 men, at least half of whom were Mahars, who fought non-stop without food and water to defeat the Peshwa's army of 25,000 cavalry and 8,000 infantry.

Likewise, in the famous Battle of Wadagaon – the lone victory the Marathas had against the British – it was a 50,000-strong Maratha army that defeated 2,600 men (mostly Mahars) of the British army.

Until Shivaji's death in 1680, the Mahars had been a part of the Maratha army. After Shivaji's death, the Peshwa rulers oppressed the low-caste Mahars, forcing them to wear a pot around their neck to spit and tie a broom around their waist to sweep away their 'impure' footsteps. Such social oppression forced the Mahars to quit the Maratha army and serve the British.

In fact, Bhim Rao Ambedkar's father Ramji Sakpal, a Mahar, was a subedar major in the British army, the highest rank possible for an Indian in the days of the East India Company. Ambedkar's maternal grandfather and six uncles were all subedar majors in the British army. During World War I, the British raised a separate regiment, 111 Mahar, to fight overseas, recognising the valour of the Mahars. Even former chief of army staff VK Krishna Rao belonged to the Mahar regiment.

Indeed, during the 1857 "mutiny", it was the Bombay army of Mahars and the Madras army of Pariahs that saved the British, thanks to the pernicious caste system that forced these Indians to serve foreign masters. Had it not been for the divisive caste system, perhaps the British might never have ruled India...

When Soldiers Never March in Step

Soldiers always march in step - except while crossing a bridge, when they are asked to march out of step! This is a precautionary measure to ensure that the frequency of the marching steps does not synchronise with the natural frequency of the oscillations of the bridge. If this were to happen, the resultant resonance could make the amplitude of the oscillations of the bridge increase to such an extent that the bridge could collapse. This danger holds particularly true on suspension bridges.

Spiritual Issues

The Swami Who was Once...

Swami Chinmayananda was once a journalist who joined the editorial staff of *The National Herald*, Delhi in 1945. He was born Balakrishna Menon at Ernakulam in Kerala.

Norwegian Meditation Technique Comes to India

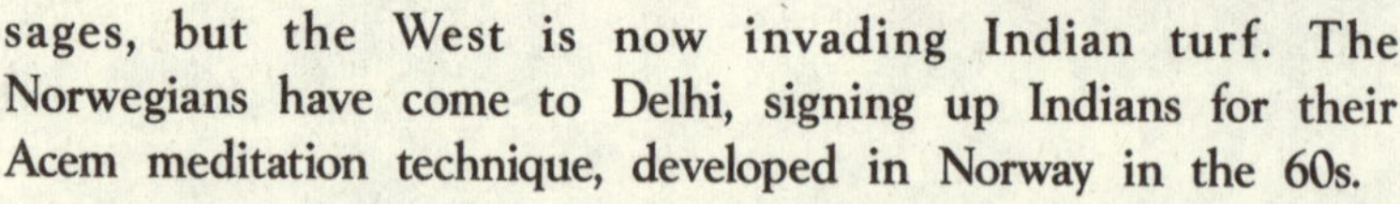

India may be the land of seers and sages, but the West is now invading Indian turf. The Norwegians have come to Delhi, signing up Indians for their Acem meditation technique, developed in Norway in the 60s.

In 2002, 3,000 people in the Capital had signed up with Acem's Delhi chapter, according to the instructor, Torbjorn Hobbel. Says Hobbel: "Introducing a meditation technique in the 'motherland of meditation' might seem like carrying coals to Newcastle but the shocking reality is that few Indians actually meditate. Acem is about realising that meditation is somewhat like going to the gym – it will work only if you do something with it."

Acem's technique has adherents repeating a 'meditation sound' in tune with their breath, just like Maharishi Mahesh Yogi's Transcendental Meditation. In Acem, though, the sound is not a mantra and does not have any meaning. It is simply a tool for accessing higher levels of consciousness. The sound is deliberately meaningless so that it doesn't distract the mind into thoughts, says Hobbel, unlike *japa*, where sacred syllables or a deity's name are chanted.

Death Through Voluntary Starvation

For thousands of years, orthodox Jains have a custom whereby elderly people who feel they have served their purpose on earth and have already attained Enlightenment can exercise the option of ending their lives through voluntary starvation. Termed *sallekhana,* although it is practised extremely rarely, even today some Jains choose to leave their earthly abode in this manner.

As a matter of fact, Vardhaman Mahavira's mother and father both chose to die in this manner. This has been cited as one of the reasons for Vardhaman's decision to renounce worldly life.

Who was the Founder of Jainism?

While the answer may seem relatively simple, with most people saying Vardhaman Mahavira, this is not the right answer. Mahavira was in fact the 24th and last *Tirthankara* (prophet) of the Jains. The roots of Jainism go back to Rishabha, the first *Tirthankara,* who may have lived some 5,000 years ago, according to some accounts.

However, Vardhaman Mahavira can be considered the *historical founder* of Jainism, as he was the first *Tirthankara* to codify the Jaina doctrines, based on the teachings of Parsvanatha, the 23rd *Tirthankara* – a 9th century BC teacher from Benares. Thanks to Mahavira's codification of all the earlier Jaina teachings and doctrines, the religious order gradually gained popularity and adherents in India.

Schools & Students

Speed Mathematics Beats Computers

Mathematics is one subject that has most students running for cover. This scenario shouldn't last for long if Bangalore-based mathematician Prashanth Anto has his way. Anto plans to achieve this by teaching students "speed mathematics" for free. This is meant to remove the fear from the minds of students, while honing their computing skills, Anto told the media.

On 24 January 2003, Anto had organised a five-day interactive session for students from various schools in Pune. The session had included priceless tips on shortcut methods in maths to prepare students for competitive exams. The workshop was initiated by the Nagpur-based voluntary organisation, National Educations.

Anto claims that if done correctly, a calculation involving two numbers of five digits each takes not more than 20 seconds – a time that's faster than that taken by either a calculator or a computer! The technique is based on the famous Jakow Trachtenberg speed system of basic mathematics. A Russian mathematics teacher, Trachtenberg worked out this technique while imprisoned in a Nazi concentration camp in the 1940s.

According to Manisha Chaudhuri, chief manager of National Educations, the response from schools in Pune has been "fairly encouraging". For starters, National Educations has begun with the English-medium schools only, but will later cover Marathi and Hindi-medium schools too.

They also plan to hold similar programmes in Delhi, Bhopal, Faridabad, Indore and Nagpur.

Schoolchildren Pen Own Textbooks

With the brouhaha over the revision of school textbooks ruling the headlines for long, it was about time children took matters into their own hands. And that's exactly what students of St. James' School in Kolkata have done. In an unusual first-of-its kind experiment, as supplementary reading material, the school has adopted textbooks that have been written by its own students. These textbooks, dubbed *Voices of Today*, are compilations of short stories written by students aged between 13 and 18 years. These are to be taught in Classes VI, VII and VIII. The students have drawn the illustrations in the textbooks too.

School librarian Sumita Banerjee says the idea is to produce a book that is different and useful, "written by the children, for the children". Banerjee says the idea took shape when children in the library were encouraged to jot down ideas during their free time.

The experiment has elicited a positive response in the city and Sanskriti School has evinced an interest in introducing these textbooks in their curriculum. Sanskriti principal Gowri Ishwaran believes that there is a serious dearth of textbooks that are relevant to the lives of today's children. What is required is literature that children identify and get involved with. This move, Ishwaran opines, will also inspire other children to write.

Going by the ideas that have been put down, it seems that the children have given their imaginations free reign. Amongst other ideas, there are aliens in a spaceship who turn out to be mosquitoes and scientists who transform themselves into cockroaches to escape the harmful effects of nukes!

Schoolgirls Make India's First Herbal Detergent

It is not everyday that five schoolgirls make print headlines and television news. But that's exactly what five girls from Pune's Jnana Prabodhini High School have done by winning an award from the country's top research promotion body for formulating a herbal detergent powder. In recognition of their feat, the Council of Scientific and Industrial Research has honoured the five with a national award comprising Rs.10,000 in cash and a merit certificate.

Neha Abhyankar, the science teacher who guided the experiment, says that her students are thrilled to receive the award. The group comprises Anuprita Gadre, Mukta Joglekar, Rujuta Gore, Sneha Bardiya and Pallavi Raikar, who happens to be the group leader. An excited Pallavi says that with a little modification, the herbal detergent powder can be marketed commercially.

Abhyankar reveals the students used a base of gram flour. With no herbal detergents currently in the market, it is very likely the students' herbal enterprise should secure some degree of success.

Lavatory Required in School, Not Laboratory!

While literacy levels in rural and semi-urban India aren't exactly hitting the roof, the situation is worse when it comes to female literacy. Even when girls are somehow enrolled in schools, it is not long before they drop out. Besides, enrolling them in school itself is a major task. Planners have suddenly realised what is a major spoke in the wheel when it comes to education, particularly dealing with the girl-child – the lack of toilets in schools!

As the astute comment went, it seems the Planning Commission has realised that "Lavatory is more important than laboratory"! Strange as it may seem, this has been a major impediment when it comes to admitting girls in schools. In the words of Planning Commission member in charge of education, K Venkatasubramanian: "During my tour of Punjab, I asked women why they sent their sons, but not their daughters, to school. A housewife stood up and said she could not because the village school did not have a toilet."

So if the Planning Commission is to meet its target of "75 per cent literacy by the year 2005", besides making girls' education totally free, it will even have to take care of such indirect costs.

Forget Classrooms, Schools Need Pools!

Queen Marie Antoinette may or may not have asked the people to eat cake since bread was not within reach and thereby earned a hefty slice of notoriety. But that cannot deter Delhi government schools from seeking their own slice of notoriety.

While government schools in Delhi may lack even basic infrastructure like classrooms and toilets, the State Government's high-level committee on education has recommended that swimming pools and gymnasiums be built! The august committee of 10 members had submitted its report in October 2002 to Delhi Chief Minister Sheila Dixit.

The committee has stressed that the State's education department should be decentralised. It has also suggested that gymnasiums, swimming pools and tennis courts for all students should be built by private construction companies on the BOT (build-operate-transfer) basis and no extra charges should be levied on students to avail of these facilities.

This Kolkata School Admits 'Bad' Students

We have schools for various kinds of students... except one kind, which no one wants to have – bad students. But even this is no longer true at the Loreto Day School, Sealdah, Kolkata, which has actually begun admitting "all girl students who have been thrown out of their schools for bad academic records"!

Incredibly, in the past three years Loreto Day School has admitted 20 such students, who thereafter passed the Board exams with flying colours. With the experiment having proved to be a success, the school now intends making this a part of its policy and plans to create a special programme for this.

Sister Cyril, the principal of Loreto Day School, says that an increasing number of students are being thrown out of elite schools. The causes for this extreme step are many. With many schools being overcrowded, it is no longer possible for them to pay individual or extra attention to problem children. Other schools apply too high standards, since they are concerned about the school's "image", and don't like students who secure average marks.

Taking this unfortunate but rising trend into account, Loreto Day has decided not to turn away any student simply on the grounds of an unhealthy academic record. Sister Cyril believes that in cases where the child is a slow learner, the fault lies with the way in which the child is being taught. Most of the 20 expelled students taken in by Loreto Day have secured a first division in the Board exams. Which tells a tale in itself.

A School for Ideal *Bahus*

While educating your daughter is no doubt a top priority, do not lose sight of other "basic" skills she will require in order to make a good *bahu* (daughter-in-law). And to impart all these skills, you need not exercise your grey cells - simply send her to the Manju Sukhramdas Sanskar Kendra in Bhopal.

This unique school gives girls of a marriageable age all the necessary tips they need for a life of wedded bliss. The school, according to a news report, "teaches young women the qualities and responsibilities of an ideal daughter-in-law, how to adjust to a new household and how to behave with her husband and in-laws".

Incredibly, all this is done without charge! The school is managed by a society called Navyuvak Parishad. It claims that since it opened in 1987, 4,500 girls have "passed out". And 99 per cent of their students are leading a happy married life, according to the sole teacher, 60-year-old Aaildas Hemnani.

Hemnani says that her school tries to inculcate Indian culture and values in the girls and keeps them away from Western culture, since Western influence and materialism is responsible for a large number of marriages breaking up in today's Indian society. While the girls are taught to tolerate a lot if their in-laws are hostile, Hemnani says this tolerance stops short of harassment. "In that case, she should take every possible step to give a befitting reply to her in-laws," stresses Hemnani.

Only one per cent of her students failed to have a happy married life, "because their in-laws did not budge from their stand", opines Hemnani.

Gems from the Gujarat State Textbook Board

What's a light year? It's not the distance light travels in a year @ 186,000 miles per second, going by the science textbooks of the Gujarat State Textbook Board prescribed for students of Standard V, VI and VII. Here's the Gujarat Board's textbook reply: "In astrology, the unit to measure the distance between two stars is called a light year."

Wait, there's more! Why is food essential for humans? Because "it helps in wear and tear of the parts of the body"! No, no! We aren't joking. These responses are real. Take the science book's response for Class V, which states that whenever the moon is overhead, it is midnight. And we thought the moon was only overhead on full-moon nights. On new moon days it is actually overhead at noon.

And guess why snakes do not have limbs? Since they live in burrows! When Gujarat State Textbook Board chairman RC Raval was asked about these errors, he claimed he couldn't comment on these errors since he was merely an administrative head!

Talking Pictures

Cattle Protest

When the Supreme Court passed an order against local dairy owners in Amritsar, they may not have bargained for the unusual manner in which the dairymen would lodge their protest – through their cattle. The photo shows Punjab police personnel trying to clear buffaloes from a rail track in Amritsar. The milkmen had let loose their buffaloes onto the tracks in the unusual protest.

India's Heaviest Turban

He may be elderly, but Nihang Naroor Singh does not let the vagaries of time or age get him down. The photo shows Naroor Singh with his huge turban, which he claims is all of 40 kilos, making it the heaviest turban in India and probably the world. Naroor Singh was sporting his turban on the concluding function of Baisakhi on 16 April 2003 at Bhatinda, Punjab.

Unusual Wedding Card

There may be many unusual wedding cards, but this one takes the cake – it is designed in the form of a four-page broadsheet newspaper! The Chaudhury family of Bhopal has printed this

unusual wedding card for their son's marriage. The "new items" are about various ceremonies connected with the marriage. The Chaudhury's have printed 10,000 copies of this broadsheet card.

Teen Tricks

Teenagers into Porn Movies for Pocket Money

Youngsters in Ahmedabad have discovered a lucrative means to financial independence from their parents. All they require is a sound knowledge of multimedia software, access to a range of hacked pornographic sites and some marketing savvy to convince potential clients that their CD is hotter than the printed page.

A media report reveals that 16-year-old Abhishek Mehta (names have been changed for obvious reasons) went to Mumbai for an eight-month crash course in multimedia. His parents agreed to this after Abhishek had failed his Class 10 exams.

Back home in Ahmedabad, he spends around five hours in an Internet café... downloading porn films! To store all the smut, he has upgraded his hardware storage space. The lad reveals that he downloads at least four movies of ten-minute duration onto the drive. His regular visits to the cyber café mean a monthly bill of Rs.800.

Back home, Abhishek and his "business partner", Vishal Choksi, convert the movies from MPEG (Moving Picture Export Group) into the AVSEQ (Audio Visual Sequence) format. The teenagers then weave special effects and 'transitions' into these ten-minute movies so that they appear as if in a single sequence.

These blue films are then sold to customers whose wallets and libidos are brimming. The duo, obviously, have no shortage of funds, with such a lucrative "business". So the next time your kid spends too much time at the cyber café, ensure you know exactly what he's up to.

Tidbits

- On his 78th birthday, Prime Minister Atal Behari Vajpayee received a card that was over half a mile long and covered 1,470 sheets of paper. In making the card, over 750 pens and 200 bottles of ink were used.
- Ram Babu from Lucknow can mimic the calls of 329 different animals and birds as well as 50 types of vehicles!
- Did you know that the words 'lakh' and 'crore' do not exist in the English language? The two words are only used in India, Pakistan and Bangladesh and are derivatives of the Hindi words *laakh* and *karod*.
- Vinoba Bhave burnt all his certificates in his youth. One day, while sitting with his mother in the kitchen, he set the certificates afire, telling his mother that he did not require them, as his direction in life was different. Giving up his studies in 1916, he joined Mahatma Gandhi's ashram.
- Dr BR Ambedkar, the messiah of the Dalits, was so poor in his childhood that the family could only afford a one-room tenement in Bombay. Since there wasn't enough space in the house for the entire family to sleep, Ambedkar and his father took turns in sleeping at night!
- India has no rabbits in the wild – only hares!

Unusual Records

Bangalore Kids Expel Water Through Eyes

These teenagers from Bangalore performed stunts of a different kind. Clement Jackson, 17, and Savio Nelson, 13, take in water from their noses and bring it out like a fountain through their eyes!

The brothers were inspired to do the feat when Clement saw a man do something similar in the *Guinness Book of World Records* show in the last quarter of 2002. Clement tried it out himself and, soon, Savio followed suit after he found his brother had succeeded after trying it for some time.

Vincent Das, their father, was flabbergasted and took them to an ENT specialist, who reassured the father that the practice was harmless. Clement's friends tried to emulate the stunt but failed. The duo now seeks an entry into the *Guinness Book of Records.*

Patna Released the World's First Stamp?

If you are into philately, bet you think the world's first postage stamp was the Penny Black released in 1851 by Great Britain. But if the postal department folks in Patna are to be believed, the world's first postage stamp was released in Patna on 31 March 1774. This "stamp" was in reality a non-adhesive copper metal ticket. The incredible claim was made by the Patna postal authorities during the Postal Week celebrations held in mid-October 2002.

According to Anil Kumar, Chief Postmaster, General Post Office, Patna, the need for a prepaid copper ticket was felt because of the difficulty in realising payments for post-paid postal articles.

Of course, Great Britain is hardly likely to accept this claim, what with Sir Rowland Hill of England being credited with designing the first adhesive postage stamp in 1840, thereby staking a claim as the inventor of the postage stamp. Any takers for Patna's historic claim?

He Lived on Water & Sunlight for 411 Days

Hira Ratan Manek is fasting – and attracting medical attention. But Manek's fasts are nothing like the typical Indian "fasts" where one can gorge on fruits. When this man fasts, he survives on boiled water and... sunlight!

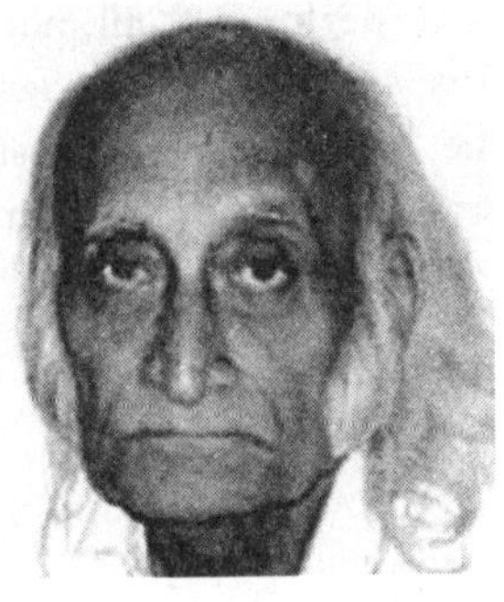

When 64-year-old Manek went without food for 411 (four hundred and eleven) days at Ahmedabad, between 1 January 2000 and 15 February 2001, the Kozhikode-based man impressed laymen and doctors alike. A team of eight American doctors and scientists, which included an ophthalmologist, neurologist, an ayurvedic expert, an acupuncture specialist, yoga researcher and a psychiatrist, examined him thereafter.

One of the experts on the team included eminent neuroscientist Dr George Brainard, whose research on the effects of light on the human pineal gland is funded by NASA (National Aeronautics Space Administration). The Americans were interested in evolving a technique that could help astronauts undertake long space journeys without having to load the spaceship with food as there is an abundance of sunlight up in the heavens. Surviving on sunlight could be a handy tool on long flights to Mars and beyond.

In August 2002, Manek was invited to Delaware, USA, where he fasted for months so that his fasting technique could be studied. The team of doctors was said to be studying subtle energies under a project titled 'Experiments with Solar, Thermal and Hydro Energetics in Human Subjects'.

A panel of 20 doctors monitored Manek's fast at Ahmedabad. His body was scanned with magnetic resonance imaging (MRI) before and after fasts. Besides, a plethora of tests were also carried out.

Ahmedabad-based neuro-physician Dr Sudhir Shah, who was appointed consultor and adviser to the US team, attempts an explanation for Manek's prolonged fasting. "Perhaps his body is undergoing 'chronic adaptation', learning to survive on very few calories as compared to the 1,800 calories a day required for a normal person."

Incredibly, Manek was physically active throughout the fasts and performed all normal functions. Dr Shah reveals that on the 404th day of his fast, Manek climbed the Palitana Hill – and he happened to be faster than many who were eating normally and were decades younger than him.

Section II

The World

Animal Antics

America's Barking Crow

You know that parrots and mynahs can imitate humans, right? But here's a tidbit you wouldn't know: the American crow can bark like a dog!

The Blue Jay is Not Blue

While the Blue Jay's feathers may appear to be blue, this is actually an optical illusion and not a real pigment.

Bat Home

According to *Ripley's Believe it or Not*, Ekambar Sahu of India allows over 4,000 bats to take refuge in his house every day at sunrise.

World's Smallest Deer

The world's smallest deer is the lesser Malayan Chevrotain or Mouse Deer, which stands only eight to ten inches tall at the shoulder and weighs just two to three kilos.

The Fish that Walks

A native of northern China, the meat-eating snakehead fish has razor-sharp teeth and actually walks on its fins and breathes out of water.

'Synthetic' Glow Worms

Paul Giannaris from Canada has invented a chemical formula that makes worms glow in the dark! This is excellent news for anglers, as the glowing worms are good for bait fishing.

The Bald Eagle isn't Bald

Did you know that the bald eagle, America's national bird, isn't actually bald? In fact, it has white feathers on its head, neck and tail.

Why then, you may wonder, is it referred to as the *bald* eagle? Bald is actually a derivative of the old English word *balde*, which once meant white! So the eagle is named for its white feathers and not for the lack of it!

Pets' Paradise

The Golden Paw pets-only hotel in San Diego, California, is sheer heaven for cats. At this hotel, cats can sleep in a deluxe suite overlooking a birdfeeder with an aquarium, a television and an attendant in a rocking chair who will pet the animal.

Berlin Artist Plans Brothel for Dogs

The year 2003 might see brothels of a different kind. A German artist has applied for "a licence to open a brothel in Berlin for sexually frustrated dogs", according to news reports. The man says it will be the first of its kind anywhere in the world.

Karl Friedrich Lenze, 54, revealed that he plans to charge dog owners $27 (around Rs.1,300) for "half an hour of happiness". Says Lenze: "If dogs can't get what they want, they get cranky - just like people."

The dog brothel would offer clients a variety of carefully vetted "employees" of both sexes, rooms for private encounters and even a "bar" where customers could sniff out their preferred partners.

Classical Music at Austrian Animal Shelters

Animal shelters in Austria have begun a new scheme to calm homeless cats and dogs by playing them classics. The Linz Animal Shelter has spent thousands of pounds in a sound system to play classical music throughout the building because this has a calming effect on the animals, particularly dogs.

Randy Elephants

Elephants are supposedly renowned for their memory. It seems they are now earning notoriety too. A herd of African elephants at Longleat Safari Park in Wiltshire, England, are indulging in sexual antics that are supposedly "too X-rated". The "frisky herd" includes a bull elephant and four females. And their antics mean the space they currently enjoy is no longer enough as they need "more room to manoeuvre".

The elephants are now being readied for transport to a new "purpose-built facility" at the Zoo Parc de Beauval at St. Aignan in France, where they will be the core animals in a captive breeding programme.

Tiger Cub to Scare Thieves

With a series of burglaries rocking the village of Selisten Dol in western Bulgaria, residents found a novel way out. They purchased a tiger cub from the Sofia Zoo to guard their village. The ploy worked. The thieves have stopped thieving around in the village.

Snake Mail

Singapore postal staff were scared out of their wits when a couple of snakes crawled out of a mailbag. A 22-year-old man will be charged for illegally bringing wildlife into the city-state.

The parcel, in fact, contained a total of 14 baby milk snakes and six geckos valued at $1,704. A man who came to collect the parcel was detained. Under Singaporean law it is illegal to bring live animals without a permit. He could be fined up to $1,000 for each animal imported without approval.

Lioness Adopts Baby Oryx

Not all animals have an animal instinct. A barren lioness named Kamuniak in northern Kenya's Samburu National Park adopted her fifth newborn baby oryx in October 2002!

It seems the lioness is living up to her name, Kamuniak, which means "the blessed one" in the local Samburu language. For over a year, the lioness has been adopting baby oryxes. She has been going to the extent of trying to protect the calves from

other predators, only allowing their natural mothers to come and feed them, according to a Kenya Wildlife Service warden.

While the calves eventually run away with their natural mothers or are "rescued" by park wardens, one baby oryx ended up as the snack of a male lion while Kamuniak was sleeping.

In 2002, the lioness last adopted a little calf that was nicknamed Naisimari ("taken by force"). Naisimari's natural mother was seen following her calf and the lioness at a distance!

In January 2003, the lioness adopted her sixth baby oryx within a span of one year! Said game warden Paul Lenogong: "She adopted... a sixth baby oryx of about three months. It cannot adopt cubs because of the viciousness of mothering lionesses, therefore it decides to take over calves of docile animals, which offer little or no violent resistance."

Lenogong revealed that experts who visited the park to witness the strange occurrence concluded that the lioness' urge to nurse young ones of another species was due to her own infertility. Kamuniak had first been noticed mothering a baby antelope in December 2001. Two weeks later, though, the little oryx had been made a meal of by another lion.

14-Foot Bird Spotted in Canada

Do birds the size of a small aeroplane still exist? Yes, according to residents from south-west Alaska. In October 2002, the *Anchorage Daily News* reported that villagers of Togiak and Manokotak saw a creature in the air that had a wingspan of around 14 feet.

Said Moses Coupchiak, 43, from Togiak: "At first I thought it was one of those old-time Otter planes. Instead of continuing towards me, it banked to the left and that's when I noticed it wasn't a plane."

Scientists also did not doubt that the people of the region had seen the winged creature, but they expressed scepticism about its reported size. Said raptor specialist Phil Schemf: "I'm certainly not aware of anything with a 14-foot wingspan that's been alive for the last 100,000 years."

Falcons in UAE Require Passports to Fly...

Believe it or not, some falcons in the UAE might now need passports to fly across borders! According to a report in the *Khaleej Times*, the United Arab Emirates is all set to issue passports to falcons in order to monitor the trade and movement of the birds across its borders. The passports will hold a three-year validity and cost 100 dirhams (Rs.1,200).

Qatar, Saudi Arabia and Kuwait are expected to follow in the footsteps of the UAE and implement a similar measure. The passport will feature the registration, the name and address of the owner, the origin of the bird and whether it is a pet or a wild bird.

The move is also meant to overcome the problems posed by a ban imposed on the movements of falcons by the Convention on International Trade in Endangered Species (CITES), which was imposed following violations of rules regarding trade in wildlife.

Falcons have been used for sport and hunting in the Gulf countries, as they are strong, fast fliers. For instance, the peregrine falcon can swoop down swiftly from a high altitude to attack prey at speeds of up to 180 miles per hour (290 kmph). Since the birds don't live for more than 20 years, they are constantly in demand to replenish lost birds. The sport of falconry is supposed to have begun about 2,000 years ago.

Chinese go Bonkers Over Pets

Thanks to Deng Xiaping, the winds of change have already impacted many aspects of Chinese life. The latest fad is pet ownership, once condemned in communist China as a bourgeois habit. And the situation is so bad that pet dogs are stolen from Taiwan and smuggled into China.

From puny Chihuahuas to huge German Shepherds, they are all on sale. A dog or cat can sell for between 5,000 yuan (US $625) and 50,000 yuan (US $6,250) in Beijing pet stores. The stealing is done because neither can China nor Taiwan breed pets fast enough to meet the burgeoning demand, reported a Taipei newspaper, the *United Daily News*.

The animals are smuggled across the 160-km-wide Taiwan Strait to China mainly by fishing boats, sometimes in sealed compartments, which can result in many of them dying. In the past decade, China is said to tolerate pet ownership, but with strict restrictions and a registration fee imposed to ensure the environment is kept clean.

Registering a dog in Beijing costs $600 initially, with $240 paid thereafter each year. To avoid paying the registration fees, many Chinese pet owners are said to keep pets in hiding.

Japanese Love Their Mini-pigs

If you are down in the dumps thanks to the vagaries of human affairs, you'll likely turn to your pet dog for comfort. Not the Japanese. They prefer pigs! Thanks to increasing unemployment and a cloudy future, the Japanese are seeking solace in their pet miniature pigs!

These miniature pigs are the latest craze for the Japanese when it comes to pets, thanks to their "sweet nature and portly shapes". According to Emi Ito, who works at Saiboku Livestock Farm Corp in Saitama, near Tokyo: "They are nice and fat, also very lovable." Ito should know – he has been a mini-pig fan for seven years. "They're really comforting and round – and anything that comforts people is very popular in Japan right now."

Originally bred for lab use, the mini-pigs are around one-tenth to one-fifth the size of normal pigs and weigh between 45 and 130 pounds. By end-December 2002, around 600 people (most of them women) were said to own these "petite porkers".

American Panorama

India 'Salts' America, the Largest Salt Producer

The US happens to be the world's largest salt producer, followed by China and India. Yet, believe it or not, India has created a record of sorts by exporting salt to the United States!

In December 2002, a 32,500-tonne consignment of common salt was exported to the States from the Jakhau port in Kutch, Gujarat. The move is said to highlight India's tremendous potential to "supply salt all over the world", thanks to its long coastline and multiplicity of ports.

According to the Salt Commissioner's Office, India's production during 2002 has crossed a record 17 million tonnes. Although India has exported manufactured products and computer software to the United States, common salt has now been added to the export basket. As a result, overall exports to the US in the fiscal year jumped 20 per cent over the previous year.

NRI Makes Every Word Count

Anu Garg is one man who has made single words count for a lot. And he's still counting all the way to the bank. For the past eight years, this 35-year-old computer professional from Seattle has been sending "one simple piece of e-mail to a list of recipients around the world". The mail takes one word, its definition, its etymology and an example of usage, usually gleaned from recent newspaper or magazine articles. This daily mail has now become "arguably the most welcomed, most enduring piece of daily mass e-mail in cyberspace".

And for weeks on end, a book based on Garg's daily mailings has been selling well at bookstores and even shot up to No 1 for several hours on Amazon.com. The book, *A Word a Day: A Romp Through Some of the Most Unusual and Intriguing Words in English,* has Garg's wife Stuti as co-author. When publisher Wiley's executives learnt that the first print run had been sold out in hours, a second print run was ordered immediately. The total print run then stood at 25,000. For the record, all this happened two weeks before the book's official launch date on 11 November 2002.

The initial spurt in sales was primarily due to loyal subscribers from Garg's e-mail list. Adding to its amazing lore is the fact that Garg is an immigrant from India who is helping hundreds of thousands of English speakers understand their own language better! Hailing from Uttar Pradesh, Garg did not begin learning English until he was in the sixth standard.

At 25, he went to America to attend Case Western Reserve University in Cleveland on a scholarship. It was while he was working and studying for his master's degree in computer networking that Garg had a simple idea: e-mailing a new word every day to some of his friends and fellow students.

Garg began the exercise with *zephyr*, which means a breeze from the west, or any soft, gentle breeze. Garg chose this word for its "beautiful meaning and rather exotic sound". Soon, "word of Garg's words had spread and he was receiving subscription requests from all over the Internet". Garg's words are now de rigueur for many people, just like the morning newspaper and a cup of tea or coffee. At last count, "527,850 people from 206 countries were receiving their daily lexicon boost".

No-TV Days in America

A new but significant trend is growing amongst some American parents – the concept of "No TV" days. The dividends are rich: higher levels of fitness, better schoolwork and more happiness, according to new research findings.

The anti-television movement received a shot in the arm when Hollywood big guns Tom Cruise and Steven Spielberg said they were curbing their children's TV viewing in favour of books, sports and the good old conversation. The average American child is said to watch television for 25 hours a week, while the average in Britain is 21 hours.

Forty-year-old Tom Cruise (who has two adopted children) revealed that he allows his kids to watch only three and a half hours of TV a week, that too only if they are doing well in school. While many children have swapped TV for computers, Cruise does not allow too much of that too!

Delhi Public School to Open Shop in America

American workers may be howling about Indian call centres taking up their jobs, post-WTO globalisation. Pretty soon, they might have other things to chew upon. Like having India's prestigious Delhi Public School (DPS) opening branches in the United States!

With 90 branches dotting the Indian map and 10 schools on the global map, DPS is opening three branches in the US. The schools are to be located in the New York-New Jersey area, Greater Washington and Greater Los Angeles, according to a statement by DPS Society chairman Narendra Kumar, who was on a recce mission to the States in November 2002.

DPS currently has three schools in Saudi Arabia, two in Indonesia and one each in Dubai, Kuwait, Sharjah, Qatar, Nepal and Sri Lanka. It is also ready to open a school in Kabul, the capital of Afghanistan, as the once war-ravaged country limps back to normalcy.

While all the previous schools were in countries where English wasn't the main language, this is the first time DPS will be making inroads into an English-speaking territory. Kumar believes that with their outstanding system of education, there is no reason why one of the best Indian schools cannot compete with the best in the world.

For starters, the catchment areas will be Indian localities. But over a period of time DPS expects Americans to also begin enrolling once they find out how good DPS is. For instance, Kumar claims that in the Kuwait branch 60 per cent of the students are locals and just 40 per cent Indians.

Bold & Bawdy

First Brothel on the Stock Exchange

Prostitution may still raise eyebrows in India, but in Melbourne it raises stock, not storm. Melbourne's The Daily Planet became the world's first brothel to be listed on the stock exchange.

On 1 May 2003, The Daily Planet was listed on the Australian Stock Exchange. Not surprisingly, it received an overwhelming response to its share offer and now plans a "sex Disneyland" in Sydney. Its IPO (international public offering) raised $2.17 million. The Daily Planet had hired legendary Hollywood madam Heidi Fleiss to add glamour to its stock listing, although this may simply not have been required, given its plethora of skimpily clad girls.

On the very first day of trading, The Daily Planet's stock doubled and 1.4 million shares were traded. The hotel touts (pun intended!) itself as "a recession-proof" five-star hotel. Just before the shares began trading, Fleiss told reporters: "Obviously the price is going to go up. It's sex... and everyone knows sex is a smart investment."

Amsterdam's Sex School

The former madam of a Dutch escort agency has opened a school for prostitutes - the Hanky Panky School - to teach professionals in the world's oldest profession how to mint more money.

Elene Vis opened her school in the first half of 2003 in a luxurious Amsterdam canal house to offer prostitutes "exclusive sales training to boost their business", according to media reports. Vis' frank autobiography, *Escort Queen with Turbopower*, had turned her into a darling of the Dutch tabloid media.

Incidentally, for the past 200 years the law in the Netherlands protects prostitution. In fact, it was officially designated a legal profession in 1988 and prostitutes have even been allowed to join the service sector union. Since 1996, they are even paying income tax.

Joan Collins: Have Sex, Stay Young

Age is no bar when it comes to sex. Ask Joan Collins. In the last quarter of 2002, Collins was promoting her book, *Joan's Way: Looking Good, Feeling Great*, and she insists that sex was "one of the best and cheapest beauty treatments there is".

The 69-year-old actress is currently on husband No 5 and claimed she was no fan of plastic surgery. Collins told BBC World Service in an interview: "I think liposuction is something so horrible – they have so many disasters with it.... Dolly Parton has a face like a doll, you know, it doesn't look right to me."

Perhaps Ms Collins forgot to mention Dolly Parton's bust line.

Playboy Wills a Fortune to Last Bed Mate

What do you do when you are 72 and willing to roll in the hay but the opportunities are fewer? Ageing Berlin playboy Rolf Eden wants to depart in style. A wealthy disco magnate, Eden received a massive global response to his offer of leaving part of his fortune to the last woman he has sex with, provided he dies in her arms after a "final, glorious orgasm".

In August 2002, Eden announced that he had signed a will with a notary that guaranteed a jackpot of 250,000 euros to his last sex partner, the only rider being that he passes away during or just after the act.

The septuagenarian Casanova claimed he stays fit by rotating a bevy of seven or eight young women between 18 and 35, who take turns in his bed each night. His spacious bedroom has wall and ceiling mirrors.

In the 1950s, Eden spent several years working as a jazz pianist and waiter. Eden accumulated his wealth operating four popular West Berlin discos over the past 45 years.

British Teachers to Encourage Teenage Oral Sex

Believe it or not, sex is getting to be such a problem with British teenagers that Britain's sex education teachers are all set to ask teenagers to indulge in oral sex instead of full-fledged intercourse! Every year, 39,000 British girls under 18 are conceiving. The highest teenage pregnancy rate in Western Europe has the government looking for ways to half this by 2010.

Sex education teachers are currently being trained on how to put it across to youngsters about "stopping points" on the road to full sex. The thinking is to use oral sex as a means of letting pupils find "levels of intimacy" that stop short of the real thing. "The courses for teachers are to enable them to discuss various sex and relationship issues with pupils. One of those issues is oral sex," revealed a Health Department spokeswoman. She termed oral sex as one of the "stopping points" on the road to full intercourse and denied the advice would encourage sexual activity.

Family groups are up in arms, though, criticising the plan as "unworkable" and arguing that oral sex is likely to lead to penetrative sex. Said Robert Whelan, director of the Family Education Trust: "One thing leads to another. It is hard enough for adults to hold back and it is even more difficult for teenagers with their raging hormones." Whelan also pointed out that oral sex did not offer any protection against most sexually transmitted diseases.

A teacher, Lynda Brine, backed the family groups' contention, saying teenagers could construe the advice as a green signal: "By following this course, I feel teachers are implicitly supporting underage sexual activity."

"Delaying the onset of teenage sexual activity is the only way to cut teenage pregnancy," emphasised Whelan. The government seems to think otherwise, however.

Sex Gets the Germans Down!

If you think sex is pure fun, ask the Germans. According to a survey, a majority of Germans feel sex is more stressful than fun. And more men than women felt that sex was getting them down, rather than up!

Around 51 per cent of women and 58 per cent of men said they felt more pressurised than aroused during lovemaking. They cited a variety of reasons: too little time, insufficient conversation, lack of affection or lack of skill, according to a report in *Fit For Fun* magazine.

Of the 1,015 respondents, a majority (58 per cent men and 61 per cent women) felt they knew too little about their partner's body to fully enjoy sex.

All hope was not lost, however, as 60 per cent of the men and women said that bad sex in the first encounter could be improved with practice.

British Capers

British Indians "Poor" Compared to Whites

The general impression in India is that Indians settled in foreign countries are comparatively well off. The truth seems to be otherwise. A landmark new study by sociologist Lucinda Platt reveals that although Britain's 1.3 million Indians are doing much better than other community groups, when it comes to a comparison with the white mainstream population, they are "poorer".

The findings are published in *Parallel Lives,* a book published by the Child Poverty Action Group that looks at poverty levels and its causes across the British population. The survey is said to be the very first comprehensive one of this kind. While the Hindujas, Mittals and Swraj Pauls may attract all the headlines vis-à-vis their wealth and prosperity, the fact remains that the Indian community in general is not as well off, despite all the hard work they put in.

Platt's findings show that an "astonishing 75 per cent of Indians are in full-time education by the time they are 18 years old", compared to the general British population, where just 42 per cent is in full-time education by 18. Despite this favourable ratio, one-third of all British Indians "are in poverty, compared to less than a quarter" for the general British population.

The survey also reveals that Indians are doing thrice as well as the Pakistanis and Bangladeshis when it comes to education, employment and general well-being. Yet, Lucinda Platt insists that Indians are not doing as well as they should be doing. While there are many success stories at the top level, the story lower down is not as good as it should be.

Britain Plans 1,150-hour Ayurveda 'Degree'

Leave it to the Indian spirit of procrastination to leave things undone when it comes to issues like Intellectual Property Rights and Patents and thereby cook its own goose. First it was neem, then turmeric, later Basmati rice...

Now Ayurveda looks like it's going the neem way. Britain is planning to "regulate" Ayurvedic treatment and training and is exploring the possibility of becoming the first Western country that will offer the ancient Indian therapy free on its National Health Service. Britain plans to do this by offering 1,150-hour compulsory training for an Ayurvedic degree course, which in India can only be acquired after putting in five and a half years! Strangely, even British plumbers have to go through a four-and-a-half-year training programme to qualify.

Indian officials are crying foul and have already rejected the British proposal as being far short of the requisite standards. Delegates at a conference in London that was attended by about 200 Ayurvaids from India and Britain are blaming the Indian Government, particularly former Health Minister Shatrughan Sinha, for their apathy in the face of the West attempting to hijack Indian intellectual property rights.

The stakes are obviously high with the global market for alternative therapies pegged at £130 billion. Ayurveda is said to be gaining increasing patronage thanks to such celebrity consumers like Cher, Demi Moore, Kate Winslet and Madonna. Why, the British Royal family is also said to patronise alternative therapies.

Joint Families are Good for the Earth

We always knew it. Now these facts are being confirmed abroad in black and white. While the great Indian joint family may be considered outdated and old fashioned, Western scientists say it may actually be a "hugely green, eco-friendly institution". And divorce as well as leaving parents to fend for themselves is bad for the eco-system.

UK's widely respected magazine, *Nature*, has published the findings of a new study that says the modern trend for a decreasing number of generations living under one roof is damaging the environment. Much more than simple population growth, it says that split families and fragmented households are the bigger threat.

Sadly, the trend of fragmented families is rising in India, according to ecologist Jianguo Liu, who conducted the study. According to Liu, "average household size is projected to be reduced from approximately 5.5 to 4.8" in India.

Liu and his Michigan University team conducted the study, which says the abundance of dwellings with just one, two or three occupants, as in a typical nuclear family, can cause a sharp rise in the use of energy, land, construction materials and water. For instance, both two-person and six-person households have just one refrigerator. So staying together is not just good for the family, it is also good for Mother Earth.

Bushism

President George Bush's Pearls of Wisdom

In the 19th century, Reverend Archibald Spooner got his name into history books and dictionaries with his verbal gems. In the 21st century, American President George Bush seems equally determined to follow suit, what with his spate of recent *Bushisms.*

Bush's masterpieces in malapropism are many. On 13 August 2002 speaking at the President's Economic Forum in Waco, Bush said: "I promise you I will listen to what has been said here even though I wasn't here." Later, he also commented: "I firmly believe the death tax is good for people from all walks of life throughout our society." A day after his Waco trip, Bush had another gem: "I love the idea of a school in which people come to get educated and stay in the same state in which they're educated."

When the agriculture secretary was being sworn-in, Bush said: "Ann and I will carry out this equivocal message to the world: markets must be open." Speaking on 22 September 2002, Bush said: "We need an energy bill that encourages consumption." On another occasion, he remarked: "We are ready for any unforeseen event which may or may not happen." At the 2001 Yale University commencement: "To those of you who received honours, awards and distinctions, I say well done. And to the 'C' students, I say you, too, can be President of the US."

Analysts conjecture that President George Bush could either be suffering from *dyslexia* (word-blindness) or *aphasia* (the inability to express thoughts in words).

Corporate Gems

Cow-space Advertising

A Swiss entrepreneur is trying to ensure he makes optimum use of his assets – cow-space included. Frank Baumann has launched the Cow Placard Company with the objective "to help boost the rural economy". For a measly £250, a company can have its logo or slogan emblazoned on the side of the cow with car paints.

While the cows' opinions have yet to be ascertained, Swiss animal rights activists are hopping mad, claiming Baumann has no intentions of supporting agriculture and is simply doing what he's doing for publicity.

The implications of such cow advertising for a cow-rich country like India needs no elaboration.

Cameras to Prevent Car Insurance Fraud

The next time your car is involved in a crash, don't go reaching for help. Simply reach for the camera! American insurance company State Farm is distributing 77,000 disposable cameras to its Long Island customers as part of a new move designed to restrict fraud. The cameras are to be kept in customers' cars, until required to document damages after a car accident.

If the programme is a success, it will be brought into force throughout the United States. Says State Farm spokeswoman Karyn Garsky: "Fraud in New York state is a $1 billion business." The investment in the cameras would cost a minimum of $100,000, which Garsky said was a small investment compared to the losses suffered due to fraudulent claims.

According to PJ Crowley, vice president of the industry-backed Insurance Information Institute: "If a couple of dollars spent on a camera prevents a multi-thousand dollar claim from going through, then obviously it's paid off. This is definitely a low-tech solution, but the kind of thing that can pay off..."

The voluntary programme began in Long Island's Nassau County because agents there thought of the idea. The 15-exposure cameras were mailed in early April 2003 to customers.

Exotic Guide to Business Culture

Teaming up with *Time* magazine, a Southeast Asian bank has published a *Guide to Business Culture*, meant to give businessmen handy tips on how to conduct themselves while doing business in ten different countries, which includes India. Talking about India, the book advises foreign businessmen to "gain access at the highest levels to advance rapidly". At mealtimes, guests are told to leave a little behind on the plate, to avoid rubbing the host the wrong way "because an empty plate might offend the host into thinking you are still hungry"!

And when visiting in the Brazil and UAE, do not leave in a hurry – this is considered discourteous. In Asian countries such as China, Japan and Singapore, the best way to establish your credentials is through your visiting card – which should be bilingual. And when handed your counterpart's business card, ensure you "spend some time studying the visiting card for a few minutes".

If in France, do not mention money at the start of a meeting – this is considered vulgar. Leave money matters for the end of the meeting. And in Britain, avoid hard sell in negotiations.

If you think knowing about all these customs isn't worthwhile, you could be far off the mark. For instance, writing in *Tales of the South Pacific*, the explorer Captain James Cook mentions in the 18th century that on an exotic island, the natives always ate their meals strictly in private, but had sex in the open. When told the British did things the other way around, they couldn't hold back their laughter! So there... when you go to Timbuktu without this book, don't say you weren't warned!

Cityscapes

Libertarian Party to Fight Wacky Laws

We in India think we have it tough when it comes to some crazy laws. It seems, though, that the Yanks have it worse. *The Sunday Times* reports that the "tiny but influential Libertarian Party plans to strike hundreds of bizarre and archaic local laws banning 'anti-social' activities from the statute book".

The "blue laws" are mostly Victorian city ordinances with so-called social vices that no longer exist or are no longer vices. For instance, in Jonesboro, Georgia, there is a ban on saying "Oh boy"! The laws date back to 1659, when the Puritans banned Christmas. Though the "Oh boy" law was repealed long ago, others are still around.

Massachusetts still requires that dogs have their hind legs tied together during the month of April to prevent sexual activity. Some of the wacky laws are meant to curtail marital tension. In Michigan, it is illegal for a woman to cut her hair without seeking her husband's permission. And in Kentucky, a man can only buy a hat if his wife approves!

Fortunately for the Americans, the Libertarian Party says it is time to make a stand against such laws and has won 300 local council seats across America on a poll plank of opposing "unnecessary" government interference. The party says it will be working to scrap as many of these ludicrous laws as possible.

Traffic Move Could Trigger Mass Resignations

If Delhi motorists feel they have it bad with two-wheelers currently being banned in the Inner Circle of Connaught Place and the banning of all vehicles here planned by 2005 (to make space for Delhi's Metro Rail), here's some news from London.

Since 17 February 2003, motorists entering central London between 7 am to 6:30 pm, Monday to Friday, are being taxed £5 (approximately Rs.375). This is an area of around 20 square kilometres. The move is aimed at reducing vehicular traffic and pollution. Motorists have protested, saying they will refuse to pay the tax. To pre-empt this, the authorities have installed some 230 cameras to photograph car licence plates. These will be checked with the traffic department's database to verify whether cars within the restricted zone have coughed up the mandatory fees or not.

The move could well cook the goose of Mayor Ken Livingstone, who has pushed the controversial move through. The Mayor claims the move will bring down traffic congestion by 15 per cent and reduce journey times by up to 30 per cent within the city centre.

While environmentalists have applauded the move, the 250,000 motorists who enter the city centre on weekdays apparently don't share the Mayor's enthusiasm on the controversial decision. One-third of motorists surveyed have said they will buck the payment and 55 per cent are sceptical whether the move can do anything to impact traffic snarls during peak hours.

Unison, one of Britain's largest public unions, has voiced fears that the move may trigger mass resignations from workers, since the scheme could cost each driver £1,200 per year! Unison wants public sector workers to be exempted from the tax.

Deserted Town Sells Via the Net

Selling real estate is not an easy task. And selling it on the Internet might seem even more difficult. But Bridgeville in California set a record of sorts in December 2002, when it was sold through an auction on eBay.

Bridgeville is described as "a near deserted, hardscrabble town tucked in a remote valley that even its owner describes as a 'fixer-upper'". But the new landowner would also be buying "82 scenic acres, a backhoe, a tractor and his or her own personal zip code". Along with his/her own zip code (California 95526) and the land, there was also a store building, a restaurant building and an operating post office.

Ed Lapple and his sister, Elizabeth, the owners of this Californian town, listed the property with online auctioneers eBay on 27 November 2002. The first bid was made barely a day later – all of $5,000. As the days passed, an international bidding war broke out for the "almost-deserted lumber town tucked in a valley below the redwood-carpeted hills".

A day before the property auction expired, bidding touched $1.62 million. The 82-acre town ultimately sold to a southern California man for $1.78 million. Incidentally, the Lapple family bought Bridgeville (locate some 420 km north of San Francisco) for $150,000 in 1972.

American Commission Plans Floating Cities

To relieve mounting urban congestion, an American commission has proposed the building of "floating cities off the Californian coast". Robert Ballard, a leading commission member, says the cities will be a significant element of a government-led move to colonise the sea. The cities will be similar to an artificial atoll "town" that was moored off Hawaii for the filming of the 1995 science fiction epic *Waterworld*.

Incidentally, a former naval officer, Ballard is famous as the underwater explorer who discovered the wreckage of the Titanic, the Bismarck and assassinated US President John F Kennedy's lost wartime patrol boat, the PT-109.

Ballard visualises the cities being populated by people who commute to work on land, with these cities being built near coastlines. Security-conscious super-rich people would favour some of these floating cities. These could also be factory towns and havens for scientists, musicians, artists and others with a creative bent of mind.

Funny English Village Names

You can hand it to the English to come up with wacky names. In County Durham, a sign outside the village reads: 'Pity Me'. Incidentally, that's the name of the village!

There are many other villages with quaint names in north England. Some of the names include: 'No Place', 'Great Cockup', 'Once Brewed' and 'Twice Brewed'. County Yorkshire boasts names like 'Crackpot', 'Scagglethorpe', 'Blubberhouses' and 'Great Fryup'.

The Famous & the Notorious

Saddam Hussein's Dynamite Fishing

While coalition forces may still be fishing for Saddam Hussein, the ex-dictator of Iraq had his own means of fishing. According to French documentarian Joel Soler, when Saddam went fishing, he didn't use a fishing rod, he used grenades!

Considering the sadistic nature of the former tyrant, this is no surprise. Soler has rare footage of Saddam lobbing a grenade into a pond. In Soler's words: "He loved fishing, but fishing with grenades. So when he went fishing he took a scuba diver and a grenade, and he threw the grenade into the water and suddenly you had hundreds of fish dead."

Soler acquired the opportunity to interact with Saddam when he went to Iraq to make a film on architecture. Instead, he ended up making a DVD titled *Uncle Saddam*. This was the result of the two months he spent interviewing Saddam's architects and cousins.

Saddam's macabre way of fishing, though, is not new. Some time after the invention of dynamite in 1867 by Alfred Nobel, poachers discovered they could add fish to their menu of illegally killed game. They simply placed dynamite charges in water and set them off, killing fish by the hundreds and thousands. As we all know, electricity combined with water can be dynamite. The effects of exploding dynamite in water are no less dynamite. Since sound travels faster in water (at sea level the speed of sound is 760 miles per hour), the concussion caused by an underwater explosive is devastating, killing all aquatic life within reach.

Taking note of the illegal use of dynamite in Indian rivers to kill fish, the British Government had banned the use of explosives in water. In the days of the Raj, government announcements were usually made via a official Notification in the government *Gazette*. In one of his books on man-eating tigers, legendary Anglo-Indian shikari Jim Corbett mentions this illegal use of explosives to kill fish and the government's ban. But in Saddam's Iraq, who would have dared question what the madman of the Middle East did?

Speeding King Escapes Fine

Kings have something in common with commoners – like speeding. In October 2002, Norway's King Harald was caught speeding, but escaped being fined thanks to royal immunity, reported the Norwegian daily *Verdens Gang*.

King Harald was hailed down when his car was going 10 km over the speed limit. The $130 fine was not enforced because Norway's 1814 constitution grants the king blanket immunity from prosecution for any crime or misdemeanour.

Demi Moore's Skin-deep Beauty

Looking good can nowadays cost a bomb. Ask Demi Moore. The 40-year-old actress supposedly has the body of a 20-year-old, thanks to exercise and a monitored diet... Not to mention all those wallet-blowing face and body jobs.

For a cool $400,000, the Hollywood starlet of *Ghost* got a "total-body make-over". The break-up is as follows: Botox injections in the face at a cost of $4,000 thrice a year; surgery costing $10,000 to replace the breast implants with smaller ones; liposuction worth $15,000 to suck the fat from her belly, buttocks and thighs; collagen injections in her lips and other skin treatment for $6,240; and teeth whitening with porcelain veneers for a cool $16,000.

That was simply the body job. Now comes the hired entourage! A nutritionist cost just $22,000; a personal trainer – $25,000; a yoga instructor – a measly $15,600 and a kickboxing coach a whopping $230,000.

As a close confidante put it, "...considering the millions she has made, it's nothing".

This Justice Dispenses Poetic Justice

When it comes to quirks, Justice J Michael Eakin of the Pennsylvania Supreme Court stands in a category of his own. While other Justices simply pass terse and not-so-terse judgements, Justice Eakin does so in verse.

The latest case that got the good Judge into print concerned a lie about an engagement ring. Louis Porreco had fibbed to his teenage wife-to-be that the ring he gave her was worth $21,000, which was around half her net worth when they got married. Thirty years older than the girl, Porreco himself was worth about $3 million.

Their nuptial agreement entitled Ms Porreco to a payment of $3,500 per year if the marriage floundered. And after it did, what should the former Ms Porreco discover but that her engagement ring was fake. While the majority ruling was that Porreco's misstatement didn't amount to fraud, Eakin dissented with the words:

A groom must expect matrimonial pandemonium
When his spouse finds he's given her cubic zirconium
Given their history and Pygmalion relation
I find her reliance was with justification.

Judge Eakin has supposedly had his rhymie-dhymie fun in other cases that concerned animals and car repair companies. Justifies Justice Eakin: "I would never do it in a serious criminal case. The subject of the case has to call for a little grin here or there."

The other Justices, including Chief Justice Stephen A Zappala, aren't exactly amused. But as far as Justice Eakin is concerned, even if they mind, never mind!

The Cyber-beggars

A spendthrift woman discovered a novel way to pay off her debts – begging in cyberspace. Karyn Bosnak had run up $20,000 in credit card debts from her life in New York. Unable to pay off her dues, she decided to beg on the Internet, appealing to surfers to contribute to her cause. In November 2002, she had collected a tidy $13,000 from generous Web strangers who responded on her site http://www.savekaryn.com.

Thanks to her newfound fame, Bosnak managed to get talk show appearances and reportedly signed a book deal.

It was Yahoo! that first began a "begging" category with four sites in 1996. But in the last quarter of 2002, Yahoo! rechristened the category e-panhandling, to make it sound politically correct. Last heard, there was a herd of cyber-beggars seeking alms for various causes, including an opera singer trying to pay for her voice lessons and college loans (http://www.saveelained.com).

Hollywood Hero Bares Butt to Sell Film

With films bombing left, right and centre, be it Hollywood or Bollywood, what can filmmakers do to make the cash registers jingle and tingle? The producers of *Solaris* decided to bare their hero's arse!

In an interview given to a German magazine, Hollywood heartthrob George Clooney claims he bared his bottom in the movie *Solaris* in order to stir up excitement and promote the film. Clooney said the producers found it difficult to sell the film since it was a hybrid of sci-fi and romance. The magazine quoted Clooney as saying: "It's a serious film without any spectacular special effects and, in times like these, these sorts of films can be difficult to promote."

As for Bollywood, the last hero to show his butt was Rishi Kapoor in *Bobby* (1972). Other Bollywood filmmakers may perhaps follow Rishi and Clooney's examples!

Heroine Prefers Kissing Women on Screen

Hollywood star Julianne Moore feels women are nicer than men to kiss in the movies because they always smell nicer. Moore likely gained the invaluable experience during her screen kiss with Toni Collette in *The Hours*.

Said Moore: "She smelled so nice. You kiss an actor and you don't know what they are going to smell like. But you kiss a girl and she is going to smell good. And she's very soft. They're soft and they smell nice. Guys don't."

Moore claimed she had never kissed a woman in real life. "I've only been involved with men sexually." Perhaps. And perhaps not!

King of Pop Dislikes Pop Music!

Michael Jackson's strange behaviour in dangling his infant son from a hotel window may have shocked the world, but there are other shockers about the man, though of a harmless kind.

In a rare interview given to the German magazine, *Bunte*, Michael Jackson revealed that during a shopping excursion in Berlin, he purchased two classical music compact discs, but no pop music discs. The reason? "I don't like pop music."

Here's one pop star who is raking in the moolah without liking the stuff he dishes out.

Bin Laden Plans a Pop Career!

Osama bin Laden may be giving the Laden family a bad name, but his niece will earn the Laden's some goodwill, if her plans come to fruition. While Osama attracts air strikes and wins time on *Al-Jazeera*, Waffa bin Laden – Osama's niece – should win airtime on *MTV* and *Channel V*.

Having gone to Britain in the last quarter of 2002, Waffa is busy in the studios recording demos. Born an American citizen, Waffa told the *Mail on Sunday*: "I love American music like *Destiny's Child*."

Waffa is however worried that her notorious uncle Osama's notoriety might cast a long shadow on her music aspirations, although her father Yeslam has purportedly disowned Osama.

Rumour-monger Charles Dickens

Who would believe that novelist Charles Dickens could have a malicious streak in him. But going by what he did to Madame Tussaud's Waxworks, he definitely did.

It seems that Dickens was annoyed that the London wax museum didn't have an effigy of his. To get his own back, he floated the rumour that whoever spent a night in the Chamber of Horrors at Tussaud's was eligible for a reward! More than a century later, the rumour still persists!

Spiderman Rescued by Window Cleaners' Lift

This "Spiderman" is a daredevil French climber who has scaled many tall buildings. In October 2002, 40-year-old Alain Robert attempted to climb the 244-metre Canary Wharf Tower. He had to abort the attempt three-quarters of the way up due to bad weather. Police were forced to send a window cleaners' lift down from the top of the skyscraper to "pick up Alain Robert after rain and low temperature halted his precarious climb".

An embarrassment no doubt, as this Spiderman is renowned for climbing tall buildings without ropes and other equipment.

Food Freeze

Bananas May be Extinct by 2013

Are you fond of bananas? Then ensure you have the plant growing in your background, because the British weekly *New Scientist* claims that a commercial banana plant has such a narrow genetic base that within a decade the plant could be wiped out by two fungal diseases that are rampaging through Asia, Africa and Central America.

A Belgian plant pathologist, Emile Frison, has sounded alarm bells for the world's most popular fruit. Frison is said to be a top researcher at a worldwide network of banana specialists, INIBAP.

If Frison's worst-case scenario were to come true, it would mean more than just a great many people missing their favourite fruit. For half a billion people in tropical countries it would spell poverty and starvation, since many of these people depend on the banana for food or as a source of income. This would be akin to the Irish potato famine of the mid-19th century, when a tuber infection killed tens of thousands of the Irish.

According to the report in the *New Scientist*, the banana plant's problem arises from the fact that it is drawn from a tiny gene pool. This fact makes it the world's most susceptible plant to any disease. Just one variety of banana called the Cavendish, the report says, accounts for almost all of the bananas sold in the world today. This is because, like other commercially grown bananas, the Cavendish is a genetic freak.

In fact, in its wild form, the banana is near inedible, since it has many stony seeds. According to one theory, our early hunter-gatherer forefathers may have come across rare mutant plants that produced seedless fruits that were edible. These were the forefathers of today's commercial fruits. These soft-fruited plants arose from the genetic accident that gave their cells three copies of each chromosome instead of the normal two. This very imbalance precludes seeds from developing in the normal manner, thereby making the mutant plants sterile. That is why, bananas are grown by replanting cuttings from a parent plant.

Sexually reproducing plants of the normal variety have a much broader genetic base. In these plants, genes swap and recombine in each new generation and the new configurations offer a better chance of combating disease. Sadly, bananas lack this basic defence.

New Cheese Lowers Cholesterol

If cholesterol is your problem, you should be having less of fattening foodstuffs, including cheese and other dairy products, right? Maybe. And maybe not, if it's a new kind of cheese developed by a UK-based company!

The cheese has been genetically modified and actually lowers cholesterol. While the stuff looks, tastes and smells like regular cheese, it has a natural ingredient that prevents cholesterol from entering the body. A study conducted in Scotland showed that consuming a small quantity of this cheese on alternate days lowered cholesterol levels by 20 per cent.

China to Develop New Chemical Weapon

While Bush and the US were onto Saddam's back on allegations that the Iraqi dictator was developing chemical weapons, China is developing a "chemical weapon, under a project dubbed the '863 Programme' by the Ministry of Science and Technology, for deployment in the war on a scourge that blights its public squares – chewing gum"!

No less than eight research institutes have applied for the one million yuan ($120,000) project to produce "a lotion within the next 18 months that will dissolve discarded chewing gum stuck to the ground".

Gender Benders

Why Women are Lousy Car Parkers

You always knew most women couldn't drive properly even if their lives depended on it; now there's official confirmation too. According to an analysis of accident claims by an insurance company, women drivers have greater problems with parking than men.

The study was based on half a million claims at Admiral Insurance, which found that women were almost twice as likely as men to have a collision in a car park, 23 per cent were more likely to hit a stationary car, and 15 per cent more likely to reverse into another vehicle.

Hold it! Don't start patting yourself on your back and tell your wife, 'I told you so!' The study revealed that men have more serious accidents, made more costly insurance claims and ended up killing more pedestrians. And 98 per cent of the convictions for dangerous driving were handed out to male drivers.

Best-selling writer Allan Pease, author of *Why Men Don't Listen and Women Can't Read Maps*, said the survey buttressed his belief that women are not as good at judging distances. "Spatial ability is one of the male strengths," opined Pease.

The Automobile Association, however, sought to explain the findings differently, claiming these were a reflection of the fact that women drivers tend to make shorter journeys within town and to shopping centres, which involved frequent parking.

Health Notes

Dogs Can Help Prevent Allergies

Are you putting off keeping a pet dog since you are worried that your child could suffer from allergies and asthma just like your mother did? Here's some reassuring news...

Findings of the American Academy of Allergy reveal that having a dog in the house during a baby's first year of life actually leads to a reduction in allergies!

A study was conducted on 286 newborns to ascertain whether exposure to a dog affected or protected them from allergies later on in life. The study found that 33 per cent of infants who lived in homes without a dog later developed allergies. And only 19 per cent of infants with dogs in the family ended up getting allergies later on. This indicates the presence of a dog in the house serves as an effective protection against allergies.

Researches theorise that when the newborn is exposed to a dog, it activates the immune system, which helps ward off allergies later on in life.

No Soap and Water in US Hospitals

If you think soap and water are the best means to stay away from disease, think again. The US Government has issued guidelines to doctors and nurses to abandon the practice of washing their hands with soap and water between patients. Instead, it recommends the use of fast-drying alcohol gels.

Many hospitals in America are already "switching to quick-drying alcohol gels to keep hands clean as evidence builds they stop dangerous germs faster and better", according to reports from Chicago and San Diego.

Microbes that spread fast in hospitals are said to be a "huge health problem", since they make "sick people sicker" and cause "an estimated 20,000 deaths in the United States each year", while infecting an estimated two million people each year.

A primary means of infection is said to be germs spreading through the hands of nurses, doctors and technicians as they move from patient to patient. Although hospital staff are supposed to routinely wash their hands between patients, a thorough job takes up to a minute, causes dry skin and is generally skipped to save on time. This is particularly true in intensive care units, where the work is hectic and the risks of transmission are the highest.

Research findings presented at a meeting of the American Society for Microbiology suggests that alcohol-based rinses are very effective in preventing hospital germ transmission, because "they are much quicker, require no water or sink and kill more microbes".

Over the past couple of years, some hospitals have installed alcohol gel dispensers beside every bed, with many more now planning to switch over.

Is a Lemon Juice Vaccine for HIV Possible?

While an AIDS vaccine that aroused much hope failed in 2003, despite the millions of dollars pumped into its research, Australian scientists think they have rediscovered an **effective** use for good old lemon juice – as a contraceptive and a **killer** of the AIDS virus!

According to Roger Short, a reproductive physiologist at the University of Melbourne's obstetrics department, just a few drops of lemon juice can be a cheap and practical way to protect women from pregnancy and HIV. All the woman has to do is squeeze the juice onto a piece of sponge or cotton wool and place it into the vagina before sex.

Speaking to Australian Broadcasting Corporation, Short said: "We can show in the lab that lemon juice is very effective in immobilising human sperm and also very effective in killing HIV."

Chewing Ban Provisionally Lifted in Singapore

Believe it or not, Singapore had a 10-year ban on chewing gum. In a landmark trade deal with the US, the "tightly controlled" country has agreed to loosen the ban and "allow those who need it to chew it – as long as they have a prescription"!

As part of the free trade deal Tommy Koh, Singapore's chief negotiator, said: "Sugarless gum prescribed by doctors and dentists as having therapeutic and medicinal benefits will be sold in pharmacies."

The import, manufacture and sale of chewing gum had been officially banned in 1992.

Chewing Gum Now a 'Nutraceutical'

Invented some 125 years ago, the chewing gum is truly coming of age where health benefits are concerned and is fast becoming a 'nutraceutical'. While people always chewed gum to control their tension, scientists now find that chewing gum is a cheap and effective system to deliver medicines.

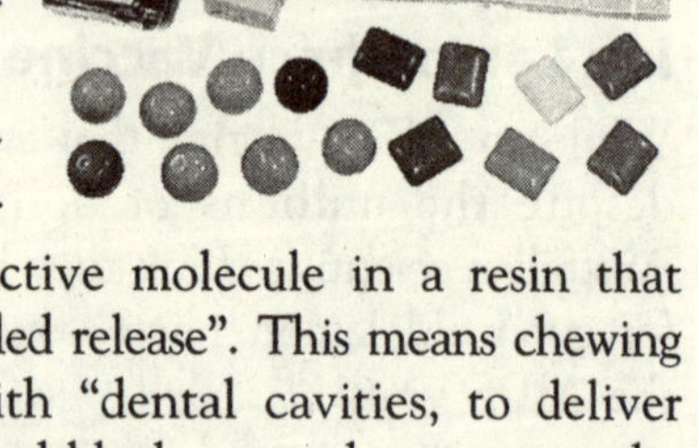

Gum could be used "to carry drugs, vitamins, minerals or antioxidants by wrapping an active molecule in a resin that dissolves slowly, enabling controlled release". This means chewing gum could be used to deal with "dental cavities, to deliver vaccines, to cure ear infections and blockages and even to soothe ulcers".

Alkaline human saliva and lack of stomach acids will give drugs coated with chewing gum a better chance to act, because chicle – chewing gum – is insoluble and has a prolonged stay in the mouth. This makes it much better than pills when it comes to pumping molecules faster into the bloodstream.

And as chewing gum comes in a variety of flavours and colours, this is one medicine even small children will love.

A Caring Spouse Increases Back Pain

You care very much for your spouse, don't you and are particularly concerned about his/her back pain? Stop caring so much! Else you could end up aggravating or prolonging the problem. New research indicates that spouses who pay particular attention to their partners' chronic back pain – by focusing on the pain, giving them a massage or a glass of water – may unwittingly make the pain feel worse.

Dr Herta Flor from the University of Heidelberg, Germany and her team discovered that patients suffering from chronic back pain showed 2.5 times more brain activity in regions of the brain associated with pain when their concerned spouses were in the room than when they were alone. The patients also exhibited more external signs of pain like moaning, when their spouses were around. Flor says that if one is over-attentive to the chronic pain, it enhances the pain.

Those patients whose spouses did not appear to pay too much attention to their pain, ignoring it or suggesting a distracting activity, showed no enhanced brain activity in response to back pain when their spouses were present.

Flor clarified that though people with attentive spouses tend to have happier marriages, in the case of an intense, isolated pain, while heeding the pain is fine, paying attention to every bout of the partner's chronic pain may only worsen it over time. "Once the pain lasts for a longer time, then this kind of behaviour can aggravate the problem," Flor concluded.

Guzzle Water, Lose Weight

Here's a cool way to lose weight – drink water! Says nutritionist Mara Z Vitolins, assistant professor of public health sciences (epidemiology) at the Wake Forest University Baptist Medical Centre, Washington: "Water can decrease your appetite. It also may help you cut calories. It is hard to distinguish between being thirsty and being hungry, so try drinking water and waiting for 20 to 30 minutes to see if you are still hungry."

Vitolins says that most people disregard drinking plain water, instead guzzling on sodas, coffee and other beverages that are high in calories. Most of these beverages contain caffeine, which acts as a diuretic and leads to dehydration. Before a person is thirsty, s/he is already dehydrated.

Instead, water is a good source of nutrients, vital for various bodily functions, including the removal of wastes, carrying nutrients and regulating the body temperature. Adds Vitolins: "Water helps reduce fluid retention and helps keep bowel functions normal."

Taking one's weight in pounds and dividing this by two can disclose how much water each person needs. The result indicates the number of ounces of water required per day.

Wonder Plant a Godsend for Bushmen and the Overweight

Have you been struggling with your weight? Just wait for a few more years and your weight should no longer be a problem! And for this, you'd have to thank the San bushmen of Africa's Kalahari desert, who are inadvertently playing a role in the making of a wonder treatment for obesity.

For countless generations, the San bushmen have been hunting with bows and poisoned arrows over the hot sands of the Kalahari. They went for days without food and water, hovering between life and death. But in this arid desert wilderness, the San could trust one plant to save them. Growing up to six feet tall, it is a green, prickly and sour plant the San call Xhoba. San hunters would slice a part, munch it and within minutes their hunger and thirst would vanish. Instead, there would be a feeling of strength and alertness and the San could then travel for days without eating anything else.

The plant and the San, it seems, will now be going places. A member of the *Asclepiadaceae* family, the Xhoba is known in English as *hoodia*, but will most probably become better known in future as P57. This wonder plant – which can be found across the Kalahari desert in South Africa, Botswana, Namibia and Angola – with its appetite-suppressant qualities is set to revolutionise obesity treatment among 100 million Westerners.

The plant was patented by a South African research institute, licensed to a British Buddhist entrepreneur and is currently being developed by the American drug giant Pfizer. After spending hundreds of millions of dollars, the company expects to turn Xhoba into a pill that will overcome food cravings.

For the San, who have been hunter-gatherers for perhaps 20,000 years, the Xhoba will be saving them the second time around, for they have been promised a share of the royalties from the drug, which should work out to millions of dollars each year. Said Roger Chennels, the solicitor representing South Africa's aboriginals: "The deal has been struck. It means job opportunities, salaries, scholarships and the right to grow the plant."

For the 100,000 San scattered across the Kalahari desert, this will be a godsend. And for the overweight scattered across the globe, it will also be a godsend.

Small Camera to Film Intestines

Those suffering from bowel disorders have some good news. A pill-sized camera allows improved detection of inflammatory bowel disorders. All one has to do is just swallow the camera so that it can explore parts of the small intestine that other diagnostic techniques miss.

A technique called capsule endoscopy, tests on 52 patients using the camera ensured a far better job of detecting bowel abnormalities than did computed tomography in conjunction with ingested barium, a standard method known as CT, revealed researcher Amy Hara of the Mayo Clinic in Scottsdale, Arizona. Hara said the camera shows the most promise for diagnostics if used with CT.

"As the camera tumbles through the intestine, you don't know exactly where the mass is located. CT by contrast provides a very good global view of the body and specialised parameters can be employed to localise lesions," Hara claimed. While endoscopy can reach only the upper and lower portions of the small intestine, the camera pill by contrast can explore its entire length, up to 25 feet.

Developed in Israel and approved for use in the US, the camera is the size of a large vitamin capsule. It is swallowed by the patient after an eight-hour fast and is eliminated about eight hours later. While passing through the intestines, "it transmits a continuous stream of digital images to a small belt worn around the patient's waist", the report revealed.

Laptop Users Risk Burn Injuries

In a bizarre case, a Swedish scientist scorched his penis and testicles while writing a report in his armchair. Doctors are now warning laptop computer users to take precautions against the inflicting of burns even through fully clothed skin.

The unnamed 50-year-old father of two was writing his report with the computer balanced on his lap. The report took about an hour to complete, according to a letter published in the authoritative British medical weekly, *The Lancet*. The very next day, the man began developing painful blisters on his foreskin and scrotum. Although these then became infected, the condition cleared up without the man needing to take antibiotics.

Laptop manuals generally advice users not to use the computer while its base is resting directly on the exposed skin, since the heat can build up if the device is left on for a long time.

According to Claes-Goran Ostenson, the letter writer who is from the department of molecular medicine at Stockholm's Karolinska Institute, although the Swedish scientist was wearing trousers and underpants, the incident "should be taken as a serious warning against the use of a laptop computer, in a literal sense".

Thai Massage Uplifts the Blind

The Thais are renowned the world over for their massage parlours and massage methods. It was but a question of time before this caught up with all Thais. And it has. This time around, though, this Thai massage is nothing surreptitious and seedy, but uplifting and relaxing. Thai massage is said to be an ancient technique using acupressure and a series of bodily manoeuvres to "open energy paths and improve blood circulation". Thai massage masters like Joseph Sribuapun, who has been practising for 26 years and teaching for 17, have now begun singing in praise of massage, particularly its side benefit of creating employment for Thailand's blind people.

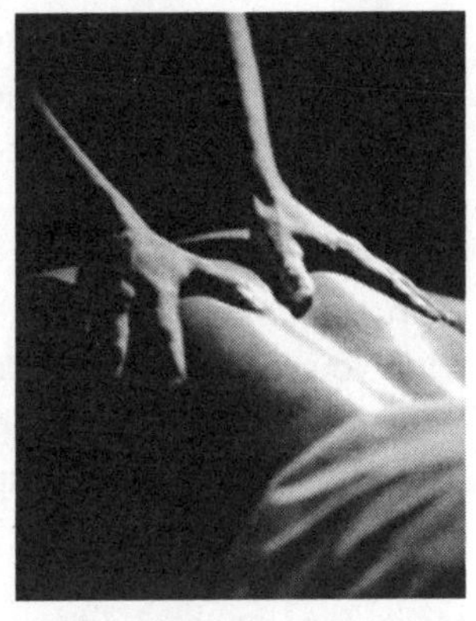

Incidentally, Joseph knows what he is talking about – he is blind himself. Blind since the age of eight, Joseph treats up to eight clients a day. Joseph uses his hands, forearms and even his feet, to rhythmically prod as he feels his way about for knots and twists in the muscles.

A 70-year-old masseur, who was heard over the radio warning that the ancient technique was dying out, taught Joseph the trade. Joseph eventually founded the Caulfield Foundation and began teaching blind students himself. Some 300 masseurs have already graduated from his six-month course. There are about a thousand blind masseurs in Thailand.

Says Pecharat Techavachara, another person in the forefront of training blind masseurs: "I felt like massage was very good, because blind people do not need any expensive tools (to perform). What they need are strong hands and a willingness to give service to people." Techavachara opted for massage as he felt it was a better option than agriculture or carpentry for a blind person.

Reverse Ageing with Acupuncture Facelifts

Are wrinkles and other signs of ageing bothering you and facelift surgery isn't your cup of *chai*? Not to worry! Acupuncture facelift could be the way out. The face has 57 muscles, all of which are connected to one another. If one sags, the others go down too.

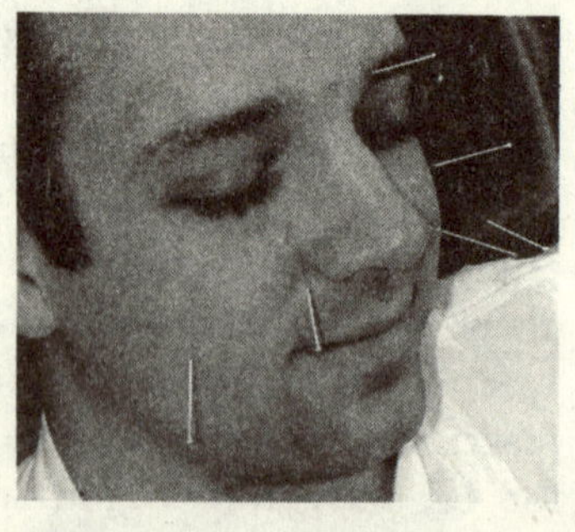

Acupuncture can retighten your facial muscles. And unlike facial surgery, you can have a couple of acupuncture facelifts once every 12 to 18 months. So each time ageing tries to catch up with you, go right ahead and push it two steps behind. Of course, if pinpricks aren't your cup of tea, keep watching this space every year…

Woman Comes Out of 7-year Coma on Hearing Bryan Adams

We knew music therapy cures. But here's proof… At a concert in Germany, Canadian rocker Bryan Adams was belting away when the notes of his music induced a 24-year-old woman to come out of a seven-year coma.

The lady in question, Christiane Kittel, was an avowed Adams fan, which is why her mother took her to Adams' concert. As the notes reached her ears, Christiane opened her eyes and began calling out to her mother.

Said Adelheid, the overwhelmed mother: "She was totally fascinated by the music and the singer. It was an evening I will never forget. I could have hugged the whole world… When I heard Bryan Adams was playing near us, I knew I had to take her. I decided she had to hear him."

Adelheid took Christiane to the concert in a special wheelchair. Her daughter had lapsed into a coma ever since she suffered a blood clot in the lung.

Explaining the miracle, neurosurgeon John Firth said Christiane's brain had probably been repairing itself. And the musical strains of Adams' notes may have done the final trick.

Hi-tech World

Hi-tech Scooter Segway Makes Pre-order Waves

The self-balancing Segway scooter has been creating waves ever since the idea was unveiled. In December 2002, the online retailer Amazon.com said it ranked amongst its best-selling items. The Segway is the brainchild of inventor Dean Kamen and carries one person standing on a small platform between two side-by-side wheels. The novelty of the scooter lies in the fact that simply leaning slightly forward moves it forward, leaning back reverses its course and twisting the handle can make it turn. So there are no troublesome gears to deal with.

Although shipments of the scooter only began from March 2003, pre-orders placed the high-tech scooter in the top half per cent of sales, according to Steve Frazier, vice president of electronics, tools and kitchen goods sales at the website retailer. Amazon began accepting orders for the Segway in November 2002, after taking a deposit of $495 towards the actual cost of $4,950. Frazier says that amongst the 68,000 products Amazon sells, the Segway would make it to the top 200.

Buyers will not receive the keys to the Segway until new users take a training session on how to master the scooter, a safety precaution meant to ensure they do not hurt themselves or others. There are three colour-coded keys that permit users to start the scooter in "beginner", "intermediate" or "advanced" mode. The US Postal Service is reportedly testing the scooter for mail delivery.

Hospitality & Tourism

'Suicide Tourists' Alarm Switzerland

One has heard of eco-tourists, business tourists, spiritual tourists and even medical tourists. Bet you haven't heard of... suicide tourists! Such tourists actually exist. By September 2002, Switzerland was apparently alarmed at the number of suicide tourists coming to the country with the sole intention of killing themselves and was planning to make it harder for them to do so.

The unusual Swiss problem is because of a 1942 Swiss law, which holds that assisted suicide is legal for people who are terminally ill or in great pain that cannot be controlled and for people who are severely depressed. The only safeguard under Swiss law is that the drug meant to administer the kiss of death should be self-administered and it must be established that the patient had made a rational decision to end his or her life in a sane mental state.

In the last four years, Dignitas (a voluntary euthanasia society) has helped 55 foreigners to die. The membership of Dignitas has risen dramatically. This has alarmed pro-life groups and even euthanasia societies in Britain, which condemn the easy manner in which the deaths were facilitated.

A Zurich public prosecutor is currently attempting to plug the "unacceptable" loopholes that permit foreigners to visit Switzerland for an act that is illegal in their countries. Swiss officials plan to verify for how long a patient had been a member of a Swiss euthanasia society and will also seek two different medical opinions. Before these laws are finally put into place, there is a possibility of many more deaths.

The Incredible Madame Tussaud's Wax Museum

This may sound shameful for Indian tourism, but it's true. While the land that boasts of the tiger and the Taj Mahal has an annual average of 2.38 million tourist arrivals, a London museum has nearly three million visitors every year. With its wax replicas of celebrities and rogues, Madame Tussaud's Wax Museum on Marylebone Street in London boasts more tourists per year than entire India. The latest Indian celebrity to have his effigy unveiled was Amitabh Bachchan.

Other interesting facts: Only the exposed parts of the body are made of wax. All body parts that cannot be seen are made of fibreglass. In fact, the model is made in parts and later assembled into a whole. This is possible since a complete 3-D portfolio is made of the subject. In case any part of the body is damaged, only the affected part(s) needs to be repaired or replaced.

Ninety-five per cent of portraits are made after a two-hour live sitting. During this time, around 250 calliper measurements are taken of the subject. The subject is also photographed from every angle possible, to generate a comprehensive three-dimensional image.

Some figures are made without a live sitting – as in the case of Hollywood star Tom Cruise. In this case, film footage and media photos were used to generate the 3-D image.

Each effigy requires painstaking effort. For example, real human hair is used and each hair is planted individually. It requires 10 hours to fashion the eyes and between five and 10 days to get just the right skin colour, which is painted. For each model, the entire procedure could take up to 140 hours spread over six months, hundreds of precise measurements, 2,400 pounds of wax and up to £40,000 (approximately Rs.30 lakhs).

Despite all this expense and effort, the displays are no longer cordoned off as in the past. The entire museum is interactive and visitors are encouraged to touch and feel.

Topless Tourist Guides to Lure Tourists

With the tourist trade plummeting to new depths, every city, state and nation is devising novel means to lure tourists back. Seems like some tourists like what Berlin is doing.

A double-decker tourist bus does the city's rounds on a three-hour cruise during the night. While there may be bright lights and sights outside, the tourists seem more interested in what's inside the bus – bare-busted strippers! The "tourist guide" slowly disrobes during her commentary, while her two "assistants" keep the spirit going with "a series of strip shows". But a man who found a 20-year-old stripper, Jenny, seated on his lap at the end of her dance, found the insides of the bus too steamy to be able to see anything outside.

The organisers of the Berlin stripper bus tour came up with the unusual way to attract tourists, after the post-9/11 slump in the trade, by showing them the city sights along with glimpses of Berlin's nightlife. For pedestrians too, the sight of a naked blonde lady standing next to the driver with a microphone in hand is an irresistible sight.

Said Udo Borges, who organises the stripper bus tour called 'Malibu Dreams': "We wanted to offer visitors something new and something exciting to revitalise the local tourism industry."

Nude Vacation for Rs.61,000 Only

If Berlin has shown the way by introducing nude tourist guides, could Miami be far behind in trying a nude trick or two? Not likely! Which is why, in May 2003, travel agency Castaways took adventurous tourists on a weeklong vacation – away from their clothes!

The travel agency "specialises in clothing-optional vacations", and 87 passengers took advantage of its all-nude charter flight between Miami and a nudist resort in Cancun, Mexico. The roundtrip airfare cost $499, with a Nude Week at Cancun's El Dorado Resort & Spa priced at an extra $770.

On board the chartered Boeing 727, passengers were "encouraged to shed their clothes, but not their inhibitions", in the words of Castaways owner James Bailey. "Inappropriate behaviour is not condoned for this nude flight. Nude etiquette always requests you take a towel and you have a towel between you and the seat."

At cruising altitude, the passengers stripped off, but the pilot and crew were barred from doing likewise. Also banned were hot coffee and tea (for fear of hot spills) and sexual antics of any kind. Castaways co-owner Donna Daniels claimed that naked travel is the fastest-growing segment of the business: "People feel safe on a flight like this." Indeed!

Kathleen Bergen, a spokeswoman for the Federal Aviation Administration said the nude flight did not violate any rules of the FAA: "We have no regulations pertaining to nudity on board an aircraft. It's not a safety issue."

Indo-Pak Googlies

Asteroid Could've Sparked Indo-Pak War

While Indian and Pakistani troops were staring at each other eyeball to eyeball during a 10-month-long border build-up, there was a chance of an accidental nuclear conflagration. And believe it or not, this could have been thanks to an asteroid!

Quoting Brigadier-General Simon Worden, deputy director of US Strategic Command, the *New York Times* reported that an asteroid that burned up in the earth's atmosphere in June 2002 could have led to disastrous consequences if it had detonated over South Asia, with both India and Pakistan concluding that the other had launched a nuclear attack.

The asteroid sizzled with a burst of energy comparable to the Hiroshima atomic bomb. On 6 June 2002, US early warning satellites detected the flash of energy released by the asteroid. Worden reportedly told the House of Representatives Science Subcommittee: "Imagine that the bright flash accompanied by a damaging shockwave had occurred over India and Pakistan. To our knowledge, neither of these nations had the sophisticated sensors that can determine the difference between a natural NEO [near earth object] impact and a nuclear detonation. The resulting panic in the nuclear armed and hair-trigger opposing forces could have been the spark that ignited a nuclear horror we have avoided for over half a century."

Indo-Pak Trade... in Afghanistan!

India and Pakistan may not be talking trade or even cricket, but some businessmen on both sides of the border have discovered a novel way to beat around the no-trade bush. In the last quarter of 2002, a 'Made in India' show was held in Kabul, Afghanistan, where over 170 Indian companies participated. This was where Pakistani businessmen and traders evinced keen interest in sourcing Indian products by taking dealerships through Afghanistan!

Over a thousand Pakistani businessmen are reported to have visited the fair, striking deals for Indian products that will be sold in Pakistan as well as Afghanistan. According to Piyush Bahl, head of CII International & Trade Fair, many Pakistani businessmen are keen to outsource Indian goods. The Pakistanis are reportedly interested in auto components, motorcycles and drugs and consumer durables.

Said Saifuddin, president of Zaman Nizam Ltd: "I don't mind buying Indian products even if it will reach me in a round-about route. There is a market for Indian goods in Pakistan and Afghanistan." Zaman – whose export-import firm is based in Pakistan and Afghanistan – has placed orders for a regular supply of Dabur and Godrej products.

While some Indian companies were supposedly in a dilemma on whether to trade or not with the traditional enemy, many are willing to trade. An official from a leading Indian consumer goods company claimed they didn't mind whether their goods were sold in the streets of Kabul or Karachi.

Language Wars

Out with English in Public, Says Romania

English may be the greatest borrower of all languages, but now other countries seem to be hitting back in other ways – like banning the use of English.

Consider Romania. Under a new law, Romania's fast-food vendors will no longer be allowed to hawk the English-only version, hotdog. Instead, they will also have to offer what translates into Romanian as "a kind of sausage in a kind of roll". Computer companies promoting a "laptop" would also hawk "an apparatus for putting at the top of the lap".

Although this may sound funny if not fishy, Senator George Pruteanu says there's no other option if one is to preserve Romanian from the ever-rising influence of English and other foreign languages. Pruteanu's legislation had some Romanians "up in arms and others bent over with laughter", according to a report. Pruteanu says 80 per cent of Romania's 22 million people are confused by English expressions, therefore, the zany legislation.

Beijing Declares War on 'Chinglish'

Did you know you could savour "fried pawns" and "bean eurd" in China's capital city, Beijing? Thanks to the plethora of misspelled and incomprehensible English words, Beijing has declared war on 'Chinglish', according to the State-run *China Daily*.

The report quoted Xiong Yumei, vice-director of the Beijing Tourism Bureau as saying: "There are many 'Chinglish' words on road signs, public notices, menus and signs describing scenic spots, which often puzzle foreigners." This is due to the misspellings, obscure abbreviations and jarring word-for-word translations of Chinese characters into English.

A few of these semantic masterpieces include: "Collecting Money Toilet" for a public toilet and "To take notice of safe, the slippery are very crafty" for a sign warning that the roads are slippery!

Restaurant menus take the cake, though. Revealed Australian tourist Janet Clause: "When I had dinner with my friends at a Chinese restaurant at the Temple of Heaven, it took us a while to realise that the 'crap' on the menu was, in fact, a misspelled but very tasty fish."

One wonders how many tourists are brave enough in trying "carp" in Beijing restaurants that are "crap" (also termed *shit* in simple English!) on the menus.

Swiss Join English-bashing Bandwagon

Besides the Romanians and Chinese, the Swiss have also gotten into the act of English-bashing. Although they speak three major languages, the Swiss are in no mood to accommodate a fourth. A Geneva-based report says: "A new government lexicon aims to replace anglicisms, mainly the computerese kind, with purebred German, French and Italian equivalents."

So, instead of "spam", the Swiss would be encouraged to say "courrier de masse non sollicite"! Wonder how the Swiss would say "cheese"!

Metal Nuggets

Silver Can Destroy 650 Disease-causing Bacteria

Argentina was named after *argentum* (the Latin name for silver) because the country had large deposits of silver. Around 327 BC, when Alexander the Great invaded India, his soldiers suffered from a gastrointestinal disease, while high officials in his army did not fall prey to this disease. The Greek Army never figured out the cause of this strange, selective illness.

It wasn't until 2,000 years later that the mystery was uncovered. Scientists concluded that foot soldiers suffered from the stomach ailment because they used tin cups for drinking water, while high-ranking officers used silver utensils. Silver has the property of purifying water and can destroy 650 types of disease-causing bacteria. And just a ten-millionth part of one gram of silver is sufficient to purify one litre of water. This was the reason why officers of the Greek Army were safe from the gastrointestinal disease.

The ruler of Persia, Cyrus, used silver utensils for storing water during his journeys. These were called sacred silver vessels.

When Iron Cost More Than Gold!

Since prehistoric times, man has been making use of iron. Although iron is a very cheap metal now, this was not the case 5,000 years ago. Believe it or not, the ancient Egyptians had to part with a large quantity of gold to obtain a small quantity of iron, since iron had multiple everyday uses!

Which is why the Indian ruler Porus gifted 15 kg of good-quality iron after Alexander the Great defeated him.

Lead and the Rise and Fall of the Roman Empire

The ancient Egyptians probably discovered lead, where a 6,000-year-old statue made of lead was found. And about 3,000 years ago, the Romans used lead on a large scale. Pipes, utensils, ornaments and other bric-a-brac were all made from lead.

Although lead may have played a role in the flourishing of the Roman civilisation, ironically, it also had a hand in its ultimate decline. Through constant use, lead enters the body and acts as a slow poison. This was supposed to have affected the mental faculties of the Romans and caused many disorders.

Lead is also harmful to animals and plants, which is why it is no longer put to the uses that the ancient Romans once did.

The Metal that Costs More Than Gold

Modern man came to know about platinum only in the 16th century, although the Aztecs in America knew about this metal and were already using it to make platinum mirrors. Platinum sheets were flattened and polished to make these mirrors. As to how the ancient Aztecs managed to create the high temperatures required to make these sheets of platinum is still a mystery.

Aztec King Montezuma presented several platinum mirrors to the Spanish explorers that were meant for the King of Spain. The Spanish were, however, looking for gold. When the Spanish Army filtered the sand of the Columbian river Platino-del-Pinto, they obtained a silvery white metal along with particles of gold. Considering this metal to be useless, they threw it back into the river, only keeping the gold particles.

Today, platinum is several times costlier than gold! It is used in the making of jewellery, airplanes, radios, televisions, missiles, jet engines and electronic instruments. Alas, the Spanish conquistadors were unaware of the true value of platinum and were only bent on digging gold, a much cheaper metal!

Notes from Nature

The Plant that Goes in Search of Water

Believe it or not, the Resurrection plant has the ability to pull up its roots and go in search of water! The withered ball-like mass of a plant is blown by the wind, in some cases for years, until moisture is located. The moment it finds moisture, the plant begins putting down its roots and springs to life anew.

The World's Largest Living Organism in Danger

Do you know which is the world's largest living organism? The blue whale?! Nah, that's the world's largest living mammal, not the largest living *organism*.

That distinction goes to Australia's Great Barrier Reef, which is also one of the Kangaroo country's prize tourist attractions. How long this distinction will last, though, is anybody's guess, thanks to the killer 'white syndrome', a new bleaching disease, which has infected 33 of its 48 reefs.

Normally, the Great Barrier Reef is "brilliantly multi-coloured and teeming with kaleidoscopic life". But the affected reefs have now "acquired a deathly white pallor, the result of dying tissues". Following the warmest-ever seawater temperatures in December 2001 and January 2002, the reef began bleaching. By then, 60 per cent of the reef was affected and scientists fear the reef could suffer irreversible damage.

The Great Barrier Reef is home to hundreds of endangered as well as yet undiscovered plant and animal species. Coastal and marine pollution has been ruled out as the culprit, since the water at the infected parts is pristine. The factor that could be responsible is the rising water temperatures. Warmer waters stress out the corals, forcing the resident algae to eject themselves. This leaves the coral "drained of all colour and life".

Although ocean temperatures have risen by just half a degree Celsius over the past century, the delicate corals have a temperature threshold that is very low. This is yet another instance of the dangers of global warming. Already, 10,000 square kilometres (27 per cent) of the world's reefs have been killed. If the problem is left unchecked, this figure could soon rise to 60 per cent, leaving the world much the poorer for the reefs' pristine beauty, as well as killing the livelihood of thousands of people who depend on the reefs for their bread and butter.

Where Sicily Hangs Upside Down

You have heard of a mirage. But have you heard of looming? A mirage is seen in hot temperatures in deserts, while a similar phenomenon called *looming* is witnessed in cold regions. On the south coasts of Italy there is a village from where Sicily is seen as though hanging upside down! This is called *Fata Morgana.*

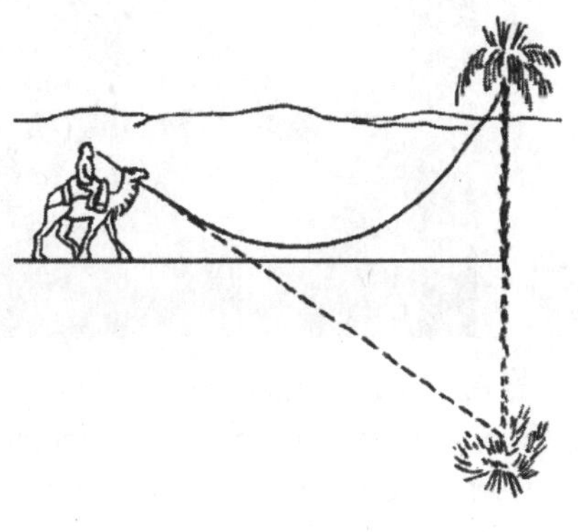

In cold countries, the air near the earth's surface gets cooler and denser as compared to the upper layers. As we go above the earth's surface, the air becomes rarer and rarer. The rays of light coming from a ship or some other object travel from a denser to rarer medium and get away from the normal. There comes a condition when the angle of incidence becomes larger than the critical angle and the total internal reflection of light takes place. So if there was a ship on the horizon, this makes an inverted image of the ship, as though hanging upside down! In looming, hills, valleys and snow-covered peaks at 120 degrees across the horizon appear inverted in the sky.

Where Hot Water Springs are Used for Heating

Hot water springs and geysers can be a natural source of energy. Pohutu in New Zealand is that country's biggest geyser from which a 30-metre-high fountain of water erupts. The natives of the nearby Maori village utilise this natural source of energy for cooking, washing and bathing. This natural geyser has reduced the inhabitants' fuel needs to a large extent. The hot water from this geyser is supplied through pipelines to a nearby city called Rotorua for heating homes.

And in a small village called Larderello in Italy, geothermal energy is used to produce electricity. The hot steam from the geyser of Larderello village rises to a height of 50 metres. The temperature of this steam is more than 190 degrees C. To generate electricity, a hole is drilled in the rock about 150 to 450 metres deep from which pressurised steam is obtained. This steam is used to run steam turbines. Steam is a pollution-free source for generating electricity.

News & Happenings

Mass Wedding in the Nude

This is one mass wedding that will attract attention every Valentine's Day, particularly since all the participating couples happen to be nude. In 2003, 31 couples took their marital vows, wearing nothing except their wedding veils, in Jamaica.

The mass wedding was held at the aptly named Hedonism III resort in the north coast town of Montego Bay, Jamaica.

Tree House with Running Water and Electricity

Grandparents do a lot for their grandchildren. But Martin Rossiter did something unusual. This granddad from Cheshire, England built a two-storey high tree house that has running water and electricity! The house cost a cool $75,000 (Rs.36 lakh).

Movement to Canonise Rasputin!

One man's food is truly another man's poison. And vice versa. Nothing drives the point home more than this piece of news... Russian Orthodox Church authorities are trying to "clamp down a heated debate sparked by nationalist believers demanding the canonisation of the bloodthirsty Ivan the Terrible and the debauched healer Grigory Rasputin".

Believe it or not, there are people in Russia who are actually hell-bent on making saints of Russia's most notorious villains. A growing sect of enthusiasts is promoting the drive through

"Internet sites, marginal religious publications, radio broadcasts and personal contacts within an increasingly divided church".

In the eyes of these people, the sixteenth century czar, Ivan the Terrible, is a wise leader. And the mystic healer, Rasputin, whose sexual orgies had a big role in discrediting the monarchy before the 1917 revolution, is painted as a martyr killed by Freemasons – a codeword for Jews in Russia.

Historical records show that Ivan the Terrible was a mass murderer who, besides killing numerous clergymen, eventually killed his own son. And Rasputin's debauchery and orgies were well publicised during his time, until he was murdered by monarchists. All these incontrovertible facts are brushed aside as wilful "slander" or irrelevant.

While the Moscow church authorities are opposed to the movement, they are concerned about the ease with which the skewed arguments are finding supporters. Alexei Beglov, a historian of the Russian Orthodox Church, opines that the phenomenon is rooted "in a form of counter-culture, the popular religiosity that sprang up in the 1940s during the era of the Stalinist repression".

Miss Drunk Makes News in Thailand

No man would like to be called a drunk and calling a woman so should be nothing short of an epithet. For Thailand's Arunothai Sriaran, though, this is no crown of thorns, but a title to be proud of.

On 16 January 2003, Arunothai was declared "Miss Drunk" at a contest held to promote Thai wines. She was declared the winner after she had gulped five shots of wine and then walked a zigzag path between two rows of wine bottles without knocking down any of the bottles.

Speaking to the media the next day, Arunothai said: "I was not drunk. Only a little bit dizzy. I was fine and refreshed after a cup of coffee and washing my face. The local wine is rather sweet… like orange juice."

A 36-year-old wine seller, Arunothai pipped 14 other female contestants by finishing the obstacle course in seven seconds after consuming five pegs of wine. That wasn't all. To make things more difficult for the contestants, they were attired in the traditional Thai dresses of heavy silk finery that included gold headgear.

The title "Miss Meri" carried prize money of 5,000 baht (about Rs.5,800). Meri in local parlance means liquor or a drunk woman. The word owes its origins to a Thai folk story in which Phra Rot-Meri, the female protagonist, is tricked into getting drunk. While the contest was held to promote Thai products and encourage people to stop consuming foreign whisky, some Thai senators termed it a disgrace to the dignity of Thai women. A conservative Buddhist country, Thai society frowns on public drunkenness, particularly by women.

Miss Drunk, however, would have none of this. "It was fun and I do not understand why people criticise us for promoting local production. One has to accept the truth that women drinking wine is widely common in society."

Will Blondes Become Extinct? Yes and No!

Imagine if blondes were to go extinct. Where would we get our inexhaustible supply of blonde jokes, which are as wacky as Sardar jokes? In September 2002, media reports said that a "study by experts in Germany" claimed that natural blondes had joined the list of endangered species. The last of the blondes, it was claimed, would be extinct by 2202. The study was attributed to the World Health Organisation.

The researchers further stated that the last of the blondes (truly natural ones) would be born in Finland, which is the country with the highest proportion of blondes. However, too few people now carried the gene for blondes to last for more than the next couple of centuries. The problem, the study claimed, was that a recessive gene caused blonde hair. For a child to have blonde hair, it must have the gene on both sides of the family in the grandparents' generation.

Less than a week after the so-called "expert study" was published, the WHO refuted the report, claiming it had never commissioned such a study nor reported that blondes would become extinct. This was one hoax that had everybody fooled – blonde and non-blonde.

Malaysia's Transvestite Beauty Contest

Beauty contests may be banned or frowned upon in Islamic nations, but this Malaysian beauty pageant was of a different kind – for transvestites! In October 2002, Malaysian religious authorities raided a transvestite beauty pageant, arresting 80 Muslim contestants and guests, according to Malaysian officers.

State Religious Officer Abdul Rahim Mahmud said that his team, backed by the local police, stormed the "Queen of Paperdolls 2002" contest at Muar, a small town located in southern Johor state. Contestants ran helter-skelter on seeing the raiding party, with many of them hiding in secret compartments in the lounge, in order to evade arrest. Of the 200 participating transvestites, around 80 were arrested, according to a report published in *The Star* newspaper.

British Employees Spend 90 Minutes Flirting

If you thought only India had many *kaamchors* (shirkers), you're wrong. A survey conducted in the last quarter of 2002 by Halifax Share Dealings reveals that British employees spend more than 90 minutes a day gossiping, sending e-mails to friends and flirting in the office.

In a typical workday, the staff spend 54 minutes gossiping, 16 minutes flirting, 14 minutes surfing the Internet, nine minutes e-mailing friends and relatives and three minutes shopping online, according to a report in the *Daily Telegraph*.

And contrary to popular belief that damns the fair sex for idle chatter and gossip, the survey of 2,000 employees found that men spent almost the same amount of time as women gossiping.

Curse of Tutankhamen's Tomb a Hoax

Remember the tale about the curse of Tutankhamen's tomb we kept hearing about during school days? The story went that this curse was supposed to have resulted in the death of many of those involved in the opening of the pharaoh's tomb over 80 years ago. Australian researchers now say that's just what it was – a story.

The British Medical Journal published a study by Mark Nelson of Monash University in Melbourne, which found that most of those who were present during the opening of the tomb in 1922 lived to a ripe old age. In the words of Nelson: "(The myth) was certainly generated by rival newspapers that were shut out of the find of the century when exclusive rights were given to the *Times of London.*"

As per the account of archaeologist Howard Carter, who had led the team, 25 Westerners were present when the tomb was opened. The legend was born when Carter's sponsor Lord Carnarvon died barely weeks after the opening. Newspapers then went to town claiming that a curse was engraved on the tomb, although there was no record of one. Nelson's investigations revealed that most of those who were present at the 1922 opening lived to an average age of 70 years.

Burglar Leaves Bio-data at Crime Spot

Burglars leaving vital clues behind can be called amateurs, while top-notch professionals leave deliberate clues meant as calling cards to claim credit. But what do you call one who accidentally leaves his Curriculum Vitae at the crime spot?

Speaking of the break-in in Switzerland, a police spokesman revealed: "His name and address were written on it and so we paid him a little visit. I assume he realised at some point that he had lost something and so I don't suppose he was very surprised."

The 19-year-old Hungarian youth was arrested on suspicion of burglary in Oberwil, a town near the border of France, for stealing some camera equipment worth 10,000 Swiss francs.

Wright Brothers' Flight Baffles Modern Aviation

India may have its rust-free iron pillar and the ancients may have built Stonehenge and the Pyramids, yet millennia later, modern man is still baffled by these ancient technological marvels. Stranger still is the fact that modern aviation authorities are baffled how Orville and Wilbur Wright flew the first airplane!

After their historic first flight in 1903, flying gradually came of age over the decades. Yet, a century later, aviation authorities wonder how they did it. At least four teams of American craftsmen and scientists are currently building replicas of the first wood-and-fabric aeroplane to learn how two bicycle mechanics with no college education succeeded where other inventors had failed. The teams hope their replicas will fly on or before 17 December 2003, the hundredth anniversary of the Wright Brothers' first flight.

Says Tom Norton, a member of the Wright Redux Association: "The actual beginning of it is not understood that well… we don't really know how they did it." The projects are hampered since there is no complete plan of the Wright Brothers, a lack of materials used in 1903 and a lack of craftsmen who have the requisite skills to design something first made so long ago. So despite computers and space-age testing systems, there is no guarantee these planes will take off on 17 December 2003!

Product News

These Jeans Slow Down Ageing

In Japan, a new range of denims are selling like hot cakes as these are said to slow down the ageing process. The Amino jeans went on sale just before Christmas 2002 and were sold out within 24 hours. The jeans are proofed in arginine, an amino acid that keeps the skin youthful, it is claimed. That's not all, the fatty acids in the new fabric also moisturise, smell nice and combat bacteria.

Said Takashi Taketomi, a manager at Teijin Wow, which developed the Amino jeans: "We have already delivered 40,000 jeans to shops around Japan and the sales are very good. Next spring we are going to increase the number of styles and start sales of shirts. The reaction from customers has been very good. Most of them say the jeans fit very well and they like the soft touch of them, particularly even after washing them."

It is claimed that the health benefits of the Amino jeans will last at least two years of regular washing. The jeans are priced at £50 a pair, which is £10 more than regular jeans. But customers, particularly women, are said to be willing to pay a 20 per cent premium for clothes that have beauty or health benefits.

Japan is currently at the helm of research into textiles with medicinal properties. The technology is so advanced that fabrics can be combined with vitamins and chemicals, while still remaining unaffected by regular washing. The chemicals are "either kneaded directly into the fibres or impregnated through a special process called ionic bonding". The vitamins in the clothing are activated from their inert state by the natural moisture of the wearer's skin. The skin thereby slowly absorbs the nutritional and health benefits.

The Fuji Spinning Company of Matoko Suzuki has produced a bio-fabric called V-Up, which produces vitamin C on contact with the skin. It is claimed that pyjamas made from this fabric remove blemishes and improve blood circulation. This year, the company plans to expand the V-Up range to include bed linen and underwear.

Vitamin C is claimed to be an anti-oxidant that helps protect against free radicals, which cause ageing, and limits the development of melanin that darkens the skin. Vitamin C is also said to help the skin manufacture collagen, which keeps the skin supple and young looking, and also has detoxifying and anti-bacterial properties.

Toilet Wars Break Out in Japan

One has heard of various product wars, but the latest Japanese wars are taking things to ridiculously low levels – toilets! In February 2002, Matsushita engineers introduced a toilet seat that came with electrodes to send a mild electric charge through the squatter's buttocks, which yields a digital measurement of body-fat ratio.

Engineers from Inax, a rival company, weren't going to take this toilet insult lying down. In April 2002, Inax engineers unveiled a toilet that "glows in the dark and whirs up its lid after an infrared sensor detects a human being"! There's more to this toilet masterpiece: "When in use, the toilet plays any of six soundtracks, including chirping birds, rushing water, tinkling wind chimes, or the strumming of a traditional Japanese harp."

Masahiro Iguchi, Inax's marketing chief, says that in a Japanese house, the only place a person is likely to be left alone and sitting in peace and quiet is the toilet. Which explains why the Japanese toilet wars are all but quiet!

Not to be left behind, in June 2002, Toto (Japan's toilet major) introduced WellyouII – a toilet that "automatically measures the user's sugar levels by making a collection with a little spoon held by a retractable, mechanical arm"!

Toilet Paper Literature

The toilet is one place where people have had some of their best bursts of creativity. And where others live to spend quality time reading. Recognising this, German toilet-paper maker Georges Hemmerstoffer's company, Klo-Verlag, has begun printing poems by renowned national names like Heinrich Heine and Christian Morgenstern on toilet-paper rolls.

For those who require longer breaks in the toilet, Hemmerstoffer is printing detective stories on toilet rolls. To ensure the next toilet visitor doesn't miss out on a good yarn, the stories are printed more than once on each roll.

Talking to Reuters on this unusual approach, Hemmerstoffer claimed he wanted to ensure Klo-Verlag users are exposed to good writing at the start of the day. "We want our books to be read. That's our philosophy." Wonder whether Indian book publishers would be interested in this unusual mode of publicity!

7-year-old Finnish Kids Have Mobile Phones

The home of cell phone giant Nokia, Helsinki is "one of the most cell-happy cities in the world", says a media report. Some 92 per cent of households have at least one, or more than one, cell phone.

Cell phone ownership is now undergoing a worrying downward trend in age. Says Jan Virkki, marketing manager for Makitorppa, Finland's largest cell phone retailer: "A relatively normal age to get a mobile phone is now 7, when children start to have activities without their parents, like soccer practice and ballet lessons."

Since companies in Finland are forbidden from marketing their wares directly to children, they pitch the ads at the parents, playing upon their fears about leaving their children unattended at the end of the school day and before the parents return home from work.

Eija-Liisa Kasesniemi, a folklorist, claimed mobile phones have become an essential child-rearing tool in a society where most parents are working.

Cell Phones and Charity

Mobile phones always seem to be attracting some notoriety, whether for their alleged propensity to cause brain cancer or due to fatal road accidents caused when used while driving. This time around, cell phones have attracted the limelight for a positive purpose – charity.

Cell phone customers have fickle loyalty, regularly switching mobile services and upgrading to new models. This meant that discarded mobiles were landing in incinerators or landfills in massive numbers, further contaminating the environment. Now an NGO has found a way out – recycling.

Says Seth Heine, president of Atlanta-based Collective Good Inc, which runs a cell phone collection programme at http://www.collectivegood.com: "With a phone from last year donated to CARE (an international aid organisation), you can probably feed somebody for a month with the revenues generated. The simple act of recycling your cell phone can have profound ramifications. The money can be used for immunisation to keep a child from dying from a disease, or you can save 1,000 square feet of rainforest forever."

Statistics from INFORM Inc, a New York-based environmental research organisation, reveal that over 128 million people in the US use cell phones, and usually replace these after 18 months. The organisation predicts that by 2005, about 130 million cell phones weighing around 65,000 tons will be retired every year in the States.

These phones add to landfill waste and the toxins these emit are particularly damaging to the environment. INFORM reveals that these toxins are associated with cancer and other reproductive, neurological and developmental disorders.

So the next time you're thinking of simply junking that mobile, don't. Donate it to charity.

These Cars Run on Air

At the Paris Motor Show held in the last quarter of 2002, a French manufacturer claimed he had invented cars that run on, believe it or not, air. The cars are pollution free, have a range of 200 km per tank and cost virtually nothing to refuel.

From MDI Enterprises, the CityCat is a small van and the MiniCat is a three-person saloon. The cars are the dream of Guy Negre, a veteran French automotive engineer who hopes to have them running in cities and ensuring a pollution-free atmosphere.

Negre's cars have a polyurethane body shell and a rust-less chassis made of aluminium tubes. Under the chassis are three long carbon-fibre tubes that contain 300 litres of air pressurised at 300 bar, which is 150 times the pressure of an average car tyre. The 800-cc, 25-horsepower piston engine works by taking in outside air and compressing it to 20 bar, which heats it to 400 degrees Celsius. Thereafter, "a squirt of pressurised air is then injected, forcing the piston down and the crankshaft around".

The moment the car brakes, the kinetic energy generated from the braking is used to drive a pump that helps restore some of the lost pressure. In traffic jams and at traffic signals, the engine does not operate, further saving on fuel.

For refuelling, there is a special tank that does this in just three minutes. Refuelling can also be done at home with a compressor, which takes four hours. So filling up the tank may cost as low as Rs.50. MDI claims that in typical urban traffic the CityCat has a range of 200 km, while the MiniCat has a range of 150 km. Both have a top speed of 110 kph.

Transport specialists have expressed doubts about the claims and until the cars are up and running on the streets, the claim would be treated simply as so much hot air... which is exactly what the cars run on, as per the manufacturer's claims!

Electric Car Runs at 311 Kmph

This car looks more like a spaceship and runs like an aeroplane taking off – at a maximum speed of 310 km per hour. Best of all, it runs on electricity! The KAZ electric vehicle has come about after a five-year, $4 million joint project between Japanese engineering professor Hiroshi Shimizu at Tokyo's Keio University and the state-run science promotion body, the Japan Science and Technology Corporation. KAZ stands for Keio Advanced Zero-emission vehicle.

Designed by the Italian firm I.DE.A Institute in cooperation with 14 Japanese companies, including Japan's top tyre-maker, Bridgestone Corporation, the toughest part of the project was said to be speed. Shimizu revealed that when KAZ succeeded in running at 311 kmph, "it was so fast that our photographer couldn't take a picture".

With a 600-horsepower motor, KAZ touches 100 kmph in seven seconds. The car is 6.7 metres long, 1.95 metres wide and 1.68 metres high. The car seats eight passengers and gives one the impression of being seated in a first-class section of an airliner, thanks to its leather seats and spacious interior. Beneath the flat, carpeted floor there are the sole source of power, 84 lithium-ion batteries that ensure a range of up to 300 km after just a one-hour charging.

Before KAZ can be commercially viable and marketable, Shimizu says they have to cross "many difficult hurdles". So keep watching this space.

LG Electronics' Internet Refrigerator

While the Internet entering daily life is a known fact, did you know the Net has also entered refrigerators? South Korean electronics major LG began marketing an Internet refrigerator in the world's biggest consumer nation, the United States. The product costs Americans all of $8,000 and while keeping the regulation stuff cold, also lets owners download music, recipes and e-mail.

The Internet refrigerator has already been introduced in South Korea, Britain and Mexico. Other appliance manufacturers are not sure whether consumers are just quite ready for a cyberspace cooler that could keep track of their food and order milk and eggs from an online store when supplies run low. But LG says their research indicates the refrigerator is a good place to have an Internet connection.

Record Firsts

George Bush's Record X'Mas List

Have you had it up to here with the countless greeting cards you have to send on New Year's eve? Then consider American President George W Bush's X'Mas card list. In Christmas 2002, George Bush and wife Laura sent out one million X'Mas cards! This was more than double the 400,000 cards sent out by Bill Clinton during his last year in office. On X'Mas 2001, the Bushes had sent 875,000 cards.

The specially designed Hallmark cards of 2002 were paid for and mailed out by the Republican National Committee, who declined to divulge the total cost involved in the purchase and dispatch of the cards.

Bathtub Screening to Lure Movie Audience

Not just in India, cinema attendance seems to be falling in countries like the Netherlands too. To get around this problem, a theatre owner in Holland tried a novel way to attract viewers – showing them a film while they sat in a hot tub!

The film, *Bridget Jones' Diary*, was screened at a theatre in Enkhuizen. This first bathtub screening attracted all of 25 viewers. A 25-year-old movie buff, Miep Dreesen, said: "It was quite cosy. Only coming out of the pool was a little bit cold but they gave us warm towels and invited us inside where we could have a warm drink." The theatre owner, Menno van Wees, claims he got the brainwave during a meeting with a hot-tub manufacturer.

The World's Largest Oil Producer

Which is the world's largest oil-producing nation? Saudi Arabia? Wrong! In January 2003, Russia had already become the world's largest oil-producing nation for the third consecutive month, pumping an average of 8 million barrels per day, out-producing even Saudi Arabia. Russia has been boosting its oil production in the recent past to take advantage of the global spurt in oil prices, standing at $28 a barrel at the start of 2003.

Russia's increased production is supposedly worrying the OPEC members, as Russia is a non-member. Leaders of OPEC have been calling for a reduction in oil production to stabilise the price, while Russian oil companies are increasing output.

Strange Queries & Responses

At a restaurant in Japan, what's the most death-defying item on the menu?

It is the Puffer Fish. Harvard ethno-botanist Wade Davis claims that a poison of this fish was at least partly responsible for the creation of Haitian zombies. The fish contains a poison *tetrodotoxin* (TTX). Said to be 500 times deadlier than cyanide, it is fatal except in minuscule doses and causes severely depressed metabolic functions and death. The poison from a single fish is enough to kill 30 people – and there is no known antidote.

In Japan, the Puffer Fish is a delicacy known as Fugu. The meat is delicious but tough to prepare without contamination by traces of TTX, which causes several deaths a year. Minute traces of TTX can cause a tingling sensation in the tongue and lips. Considering the deadly poison, the fish has to be prepared with due care to avoid poisoning. Perhaps it is the thrill of death that adds to the Fugu's status as a delicacy.

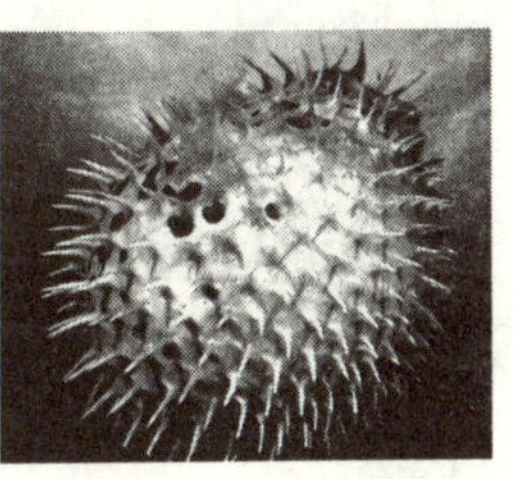

Even foreigners in Japan have to run the risk of eating Fugu. Take the case of Yves Carcelle, president of French fashion house Louis Vuitton, who mentions the things he has to do to swing deals. Says Carcelle: "I was negotiating in Japan with the head of a department store for four months… I have swum in a bath naked, with other CEOs. I have eaten the dangerous Fugu… if you refuse these cultural aspects, you risk not completing the negotiations."

Which is the most bacteria-laden object in the household?

It isn't the toilet bowl or a wet dishrag – it's the human body, says Cornell microbiologist Stephen H Zinder. The body harbours millions of bacteria per square cm in moister skin areas like the armpits.

Our mouths too harbour billions of bacteria growing on the teeth as plaque, or between our teeth and gums. And our large intestines contain 100 trillion bacterial cells, roughly the number of cells that make up our own bodies!

There is no cause for concern though, says Zinder, since most 'micro-flora' are our friends and help keep the bad bacteria (pathogens) at bay. In fact, insufficient exposure to microbes in the early years may predispose humans to allergies and asthma later on. However, one still needs to brush and floss one's teeth, since too many bacteria can cause cavities and gum disease.

Is it only mammals that flatulate (pass wind)?

At least some cold-blooded animals do pass gas from the vent/cloaca/rectum, though the sounds won't be like a mammal breaking wind, says Barbara Shields, Ph.D., Department of Fisheries and Wildlife, Oregon State University. But it can certainly smell just as bad, or worse!

In many species, this is part of the faecal evacuation process as ingested air escapes. Pet fish fed dried pellets often pass a lot of gas. Digestive breakdown of foods by gut bacteria can result in the very smelly flatulence of reptiles, especially snakes.

Did you know that anthropologists learn about ancient peoples from coprolites (fossilised excreta)?

Coprolites are fossilised human dung sifted from the soils of caves, shelters and tombs, which hold clues about how prehistoric man ate and lived, reveals Paul Spinrad in *Research Guide to Bodily Fluids*.

Early last century, researchers simply broke apart coprolites. By the 1950s, rehydration became popular, with deposits being "soaked, sliced, separated, centrifuged, sniffed, sieved, stained and smeared on slides". The lab would then analyse the foods involved – such as the chemical composition, pollen, parasites, etc.

Fibrous vegetable matter, insects, meat with bone chips, even human flesh (cannibalism) can all be clearly identified. Food preparation – grit indicates milling, charcoal means parching or roasting – can also be copro-read. For researchers, this is serious business, says Spinrad. One 100-year-old stool displayed at the Archaeological Resource Centre in York, England, was thought to be in "mint condition" and valued at £20,000 (approximately Rs.1.5 million).

Which of these is the strongest material made by an animal: (a) turtle-shell (b) rhino horn (c) oyster pearl (d) spider silk?

It is spider silk! This fact first came to light in 1881, when physician George Emery Goodfellow noticed, upon examining the body of a man who was gunned down, that his silk handkerchief protruded from the wound, reveals *Science News*. When Goodfellow removed the handkerchief by tugging it through ripped flesh and broken ribs, the bullet lay wrapped within the untorn silk cloth, he wrote in his article, 'Notes on the Impenetrability of Silk to Bullets'.

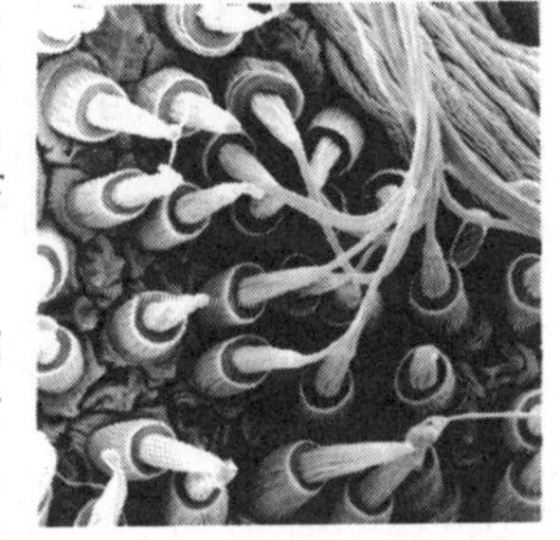

Early on, silkworms spinning cocoons provided tough materials for parachutes, pantaloons, and the like. Recent research indicates that spider silk is even superior for tasks such as warding off projectiles. "Dragline silk is the strongest animal-stuff there is," says molecular biologist Randy Lewis from the University of Wyoming. These are the threads that spiders dangle from and use in their outer-web framework.

Dragline silk is at least three times stronger than Kevlar, the DuPont material used in bulletproof vests, says Lewis. A one-inch diameter "rope" of this silk, if it could be woven using millions and millions of strands, could stop a jet landing on an aircraft carrier. But since spiders are hard to farm (they tend to eat each other!), it is not possible to collect enough of this silk for commercial use. However, thanks to genetic engineering, a Canadian company is now producing the dragline protein in goat's milk!

Some blind people can "see" in their dreams. Similarly, can deaf people "hear" in their dreams?

It would depend on when the hearing loss occurred, the degree of the loss, whether the person grew up with hearing or deaf parents, and a host of other factors, says psychologist Robert Lee Williams of Gallaudet University.

There is no "typical" deaf person. "Given that caveat, I can tell you some of my deaf students report hearing and talking in their dreams. Others use sign language. I might add that as a hearing person, I have had dreams in sign language too. Apparently in dreams, all things are possible," says Williams.

If a person is born deaf and never hears, there will be no sounds or voices stored in memory for conjuring in the dream world, paralleling the experience of the blind. But having once heard, in his book *Deafness*, David Wright describes how he continued to hear "phantasmal voices" for the first year or two, just as the adventitiously blind continue to dream in images for a time, until these start to fade in vividness.

•

Science & Technology

Cell Phone Tooth

James Auger and Jimmy Loizeau, two British researchers, have made a phone tooth – a cell phone fitted molar that can receive phone calls! The signals are converted into vibrations that travel from your tooth to the skull to the inner ear, where you can hear them.

The Dog Sound Interpreter

At times, you could have sworn your dog was trying to tell you something, but never figured out what, right? You need not worry any more. Japanese toy-maker Takara has come out with a radio microphone that you can attach to your dog's collar and have the dog sounds interpreted in a handheld receiver. The cost? Just $120 (approximately Rs.5,700 only)!

Animal behaviourists have interpreted the dog noises stored in a database, which were collected over a period of time. Each yelp, yip, woof or whine of a dog was read into and translated. There are six emotional categories for these dog sounds: happiness, sadness, frustration, anger, assertion and desire.

Named *Bowlingual*, Tokyo-based Takara said the interpreter had already sold 300,000 units in the six months up to March 2003 and was all set to enter the South Korean and American markets. With America having around 67 million dogs (six times the number in Japan), Takara hopes to make a killing in the States.

Humans Could One Day Re-grow Organs

Recall the lizard that you swatted with the flyswatter when you were a little tyke? The lizard managed to flee in one direction – leaving a wriggling tail behind, which made you flee in the other direction! Months later, if you were observant enough to recognise the same lizard (if that were possible!), you'd find it had re-grown its tail.

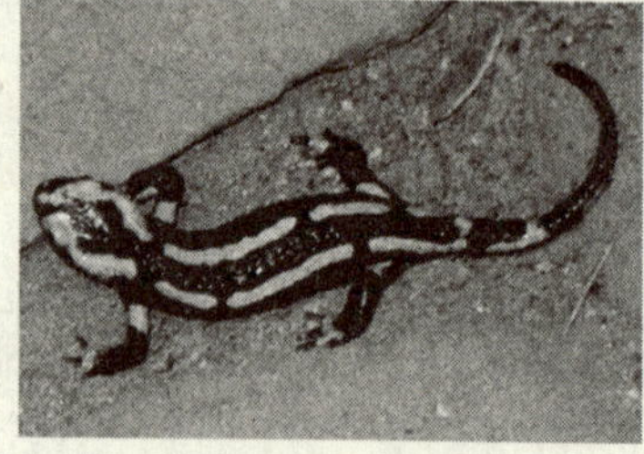

Like lizards, salamanders are also masters of regeneration. Salamanders are currently being used at the Leg Lab in Irvine, United States. The strangely named lab is because the animals here will have a leg cut off. The salamanders recover quickly, with new limbs growing back within weeks.

In fact, when it comes to regeneration, salamanders can be considered superstars, because they can re-grow "not only limbs but tails, parts of their hearts and the retinas and lenses of their eyes". Although humans cannot do any of these, scientists are hopeful that once their secret is uncovered humans may be able to do the same!

Says Dr David M Gardiner (a biologist running the laboratory at the University of California in Irvine with Dr Susan V Bryant, the dean of the biological sciences wing): "I really do believe it's just a matter of time before you're going to regenerate an arm or at least a finger. I'd like to see that in my lifetime."

Regenerative medicine is a hot topic in some medical circles, with attention focusing on stem cells. The attempt is to re-grow stem cells outside the body, turn them into particular types of tissue and transplant them into patients.

There are other scientists who theorise that a better approach is to induce the same regeneration in people occurring in salamanders and other creatures. They believe that natural regeneration, accomplished either through drugs or genes, might be easier than transplanting. With the tissue being the patients' own, the problem of rejection is also obviated.

If the salamanders' tricks cannot be duplicated in humans, scientists still believe that studying these creatures could provide vital clues for stem cell scientists.

Yet, natural regeneration hasn't made much headway, although scientists have been studying it for 200 years. This is a fact that Dr Catherine Tsilfidis, assistant professor at the University of Ottawa Eye Institute, readily admits. Dr Tsilfidis is studying regeneration in newts.

With the sustained interest from scientists and with venture capitalists recently having invested $9 million in starting the first company that attempts to replicate natural regeneration in people, there is an outside chance that Dr Gardiner might just about see his dream realised during his lifetime.

This Material Shrinks When Heated

Materials expand when heated, right? Not if you're talking of zirconium. This extremely unusual chemical compound is being touted as a "godsend for dentists, chefs and even Formula One drivers" because it defies the laws of physics by shrinking, not expanding, when heated.

The ores of zirconium have actually been known since ancient times by such names as jargon, jacinth and hyacinth. But one of the element's several compounds, zirconium tungstate, recently amazed the scientific world by its weird behaviour. This behaviour can be used to solve everyday problems. For instance, erratic fluctuations in temperature can crack a plate. A ceramic dish removed from the freezer and placed in a hot oven splits apart because some parts heat up and expand faster than others. Such problems could be solved with zirconium tungstate, a blend of zirconium, tungsten and oxygen, which is non-toxic.

The news could mean a lot in tackling problems in electronics, metallurgy and ceramics. It could also eliminate distortions in optical applications such as telescopes and laser devices where very low thermal expansion is required so that precise focusing is not lost with temperature fluctuations. The discovery could also make a crucial difference in silicon chips, which are used in modern electronic circuitry.

Our Close Relative, the Mouse

We all know that humans are closely related to apes. The fact is we are also closely related to mice, much more closely than we think. In December 2002, scientists published the genetic blueprint of the mouse, which shows there isn't much difference between mice and men. Both species have around 30,000 genes, many of them similar. And 90 per cent of the genes linked to diseases in humans are similar to ones found in mice.

The story doesn't end there. According to Dr Jane Rogers from the Wellcome Trust Sanger Institute, Cambridge, England: "We share 99 per cent of our genes with mice, and we even have the genes that could make a tail."

A consortium of scientists worldwide, including Rogers, collaborated on the genome (a complete list of coded instructions to make a mouse), which was published in *Nature*, the nature science journal. By comparing the two genomes (the human genome was sequenced two years ago), researchers have currently identified 1,200 new human genes and 9,000 new mouse genes. Incredibly, there are only 300 genes unique to either living being, buttressing the fact that the mouse is the ideal model for studying human diseases and testing new treatments.

The proximity between man and mouse could be because both mice and men share a common ancestor, a creature said to be the size of a small rat that lived between 75 and 125 million years ago, during the age of the dinosaurs.

Though the mouse genome is some 14 per cent smaller than the human one, about 40 per cent of the two genomes can be directly aligned with each other.

Bacteria Communicate with Each Other

Believe it or not, scientists in St. Louis have discovered that bacteria talk to one another constantly, even cooperating in the construction of intricate communities called biofilms, permitting them to thrive in ways that would not have been possible as single-celled individuals. It is these bustling bacterial cities that often create debilitating or life-threatening infections within the human body.

Scorpion Venom Can Save Cancer Patients

Humans once had to beware of the scorpion's painful sting, which could even result in death. But the venom of the Israeli Yellow Scorpion could help save the lives of cancer patients. For starters, this scorpion's venom is not fatal, just painful.

Doctors inject a copy of the toxin directly into the brain of the patient just prior to radiation therapy. The toxin doesn't kill the tumour cells – it simply clings to them. Once the cells are bound in this toxic embrace, the radioactivity kills them.

Eight patients have undergone the experimental treatment. Except for one, all the rest are alive and kicking.

Blue Roses in the Offing

You may have heard of roses in a variety of unusual colours, but there's one colour that's missing despite the best efforts of rose breeders for centuries – a genuinely blue rose.

This drawback could be rectified in the coming years, thanks to scientists at the Vanderbilt University School of Medicine, who stumbled upon a human protein, while studying how drugs metabolise in the liver, that may play a critical role in creating the first blue rose. Working in the lab of biochemist F Peter Guengerich, Elizabeth Gillam one day came up "with a flask full of bacteria that she had turned blue with an enzyme taken from a patient's liver".

Technological breakthroughs may also ensure that the sweet fragrance of roses is restored, since generations of commercial breeding has led to roses that, although beautiful, happen to be bland-smelling.

Sports

No More Battle of the Sexes for Serena Williams

Remember the time when tennis legend Billie Jean King had a battle of the sexes match with a male tennis player and ended up biting the dust? A couple of decades later along came the Williams sisters, Venus and Serena, claiming they could win a match against a male player. This seemed a good proposition, considering the sisters were beating the pants, er… skirts, off their opponents.

So Serena Williams played a one-set match against 203rd ranked German player Karsten Braasch, a chain-smoker in the twilight of his career. The German whipped Serena 6-1, even as you were wondering Karsten Braasch who? Venus had a more respectable score, losing to the German 6-2.

That was some five years ago. When Serena Williams won the Australian Open on 25 January 2003, she was reminded of the William sisters' Battle of the Sexes. Would she be interested in something similar again? A wiser Serena responded: "I'm here to play women's tennis. I'm a lady."

Although some may think otherwise on seeing Serena's muscular arms, her comment put paid to Braasch's chances of coming out of retirement, even for one lousy set!

Cricket is War

Cricket is now a battle of attrition or a verbal war, especially if India-Pakistan or Australia-England face off. Reports indicate that the South African cricket team prepared to lift the World Cup 2003 by undergoing three days of commando-type motivational and psychological drills. The 15 players were divided into groups and blindfolded, then flown by helicopter to a forest in Drakenberg. Each group was armed with pencil, a balloon, a compass and a two-way radio for emergencies. After landing in the forest, the blindfolds were removed and the groups went their way at 10-minute intervals to identify five checkpoint markers hidden in the forests and hills over a 10-km course.

Despite the heavy training, South Africa failed to make even the Super Six Stage, leave alone lift the World Cup. Next time around, perhaps the South African authorities will consider training the players with bat and ball!

Talking Pictures

Chinese Police Wield the Net Gun

The Net Gun is a handy device for the police. In this photo, a Chinese policeman from Guangzhou demonstrates the use of the Net Gun. Shaped like a baton, the Net Gun is a non-lethal device that can be installed on an assault rifle. It contains pressurised air that helps project a net up to a distance of about 10 metres.

Forehead Advertising

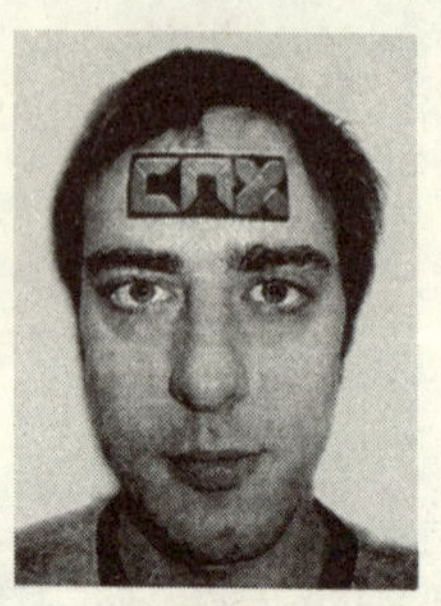

University students have a new way to make some easy money – renting space on their foreheads! A British marketing agency has begun renting foreign space from students, who will have logos semi-permanently tattooed on their foreheads, for which they will be paid $6.85 (approximately Rs.330) an hour for three hours – the amount of time they are thought to be up and about.

Canine General Managers

You may have seen many intimidating general managers, but these two general managers at Japanese clothing maker Naigai Co Ltd's dog fashion division will floor you with their silent charm! The photo shows Momo and Chilly welcoming customers to the showroom in Tokyo.

Tidbits

Strange But True...

- A duck's quack does not echo.
- Snails can sleep for up to three years.
- Swallows eat, drink and mate while flying.
- Butterflies actually "taste" with their feet.
- Although butterflies themselves cannot produce any sounds, they have the most powerful hearing on earth, up to 100,000 Hz!
- Elephants are the only animals that cannot jump.
- Sumo wrestlers of Japan attain their great size and weight by eating a high-protein seafood diet.

- Whenever judges pass a death sentence, they break the nib of the pen, ensuring it is not used again.
- In Tokyo, a bicycle is faster than a car for most trips of less than 50 minutes!
- Should there be a crash, Prince Charles and Prince William never travel on the same airplane as a precaution!
- The Mona Lisa has no eyebrows. It was the fashion in Renaissance Florence to shave them off!
- The most popular first name in the world is Muhammad.
- Tourists visiting Iceland should know that tipping at a restaurant is considered an insult!
- Until the nineteenth century, solid blocks of tea were used as money in Siberia!

- Not all rabbits have upright ears – for instance, the lop-eared dwarf rabbit.
- The Nobel Peace Prize medal depicts three naked men with their hands on each other's shoulders!
- A lightning bolt generates temperatures five times hotter than those found at the sun's surface!
- It takes glass one million years to decompose, which means it never wears out and can be recycled an infinite amount of times!
- Forest fires move faster uphill than downhill!
- Bears can run faster uphill than downhill!

Vocations & Careers

Eyebrow Threading a Marvel in Europe

There is some good news for Indian beauticians seeking to migrate to Europe. What Indian women take for granted here – threading or the Indian technique of shaping eyebrows – is supposedly raising the eyebrows of women in Europe.

Believe it or not, Vaishaly Patel of London specialises in eyebrow grooming of the rich and famous – and has a three-month waiting list, despite her hefty fees. In India, eyebrow grooming is one of the basics in beauty treatment, earning beauticians as little as Rs.5 or Rs.10 per customer.

In the words of a dedicated beauty columnist: "Threading is a weird and wonderful Indian hair-removal technique in which a slip knot of strengthened cotton is run along an area, deftly whisking away hairs at the root." The result, the columnist reports, is "elegant, naturally poised sweeps". Indian beauticians reading this item will surely get ideas about minting moolah abroad purely through threading, something they could never dream of in India.

The Great Brain Robbery

We'd heard about the legendary Indian brain drain, but never guessed things could come to such a pass. Although India has over a billion people, the country has barely 3,000 psychiatrists. Even that figure could shrink, going by media reports.

Some Indian psychiatrists are planning to pack their bags and head West. Senior psychiatrists are moving abroad to the UK, Australia and New Zealand, amongst other nations. The most aggressive recruiter in this real Indian brain drain is the UK's

National Health Service. In the first quarter of 2003, the NHS organised a week-long, all-expenses-paid trip to London for Indian psychiatrists to interview them for an international fellowship programme.

Though the fellowships are for two years only, many professionals who were interviewed said they were considering settling down in the UK. Said consultant psychiatrist Dr Harish Shetty: "The bottomline is that there are not enough psychiatrists in the UK and the British Government is trying to fill the vacuum."

The biggest lure for Indian psychiatrists is the package – over £80,000 (approximately Rs.6 million) a year – and better working conditions.

Plumbing a Lucrative Career Option

Are you just out of college and wondering what profession to take up when you get into the United Kingdom? Here's one watertight option – become a plumber.

We are serious! Plumbing is now a lucrative option in many countries, including the United Kingdom. Robert Burgon, director of the British Plumbing Employers' Council, reveals that plumbers are being sought as highly skilled professionals.

It seems that for the past couple of decades, the tribe of plumbers has stagnated at just 10,000, despite the rising demand, which is pegged at 30,000 qualified plumbers in five years' time. However, with barely 1,000 qualifying every year, this shortfall is hardly likely to be met.

As people pay closer attention to their taps (or faucets, if you please!), bathrooms, kitchens and toilets "with digitalised central heating and electronic gadgetry", plumbing as a profession has surely come of age.

Plastic Surgeons Boosted by Silicon Valley Slump

Strange as this may sound, it's true – the slump in Silicon Valley has been good news for plastic surgeons. With many IT professionals out of jobs and currently looking for openings, many of these people are going in for face-lifts and eye jobs before they venture back into the increasingly difficult job market.

A media report indicates that in recent months nearly half the patients at the cosmetic surgery clinic of the Stanford Medical Centre have been IT employees. Says plastic surgeon Dr David Apfelberg, explaining this trend: "They're going back in the job market, competing with younger people."

One female employee claimed she was scheduling cosmetic surgery for her eyes in anticipation that her company would be closing down. As Maria, a 39-year-old sales professional, put it: "I know if I go apply for a job anywhere and I look the way I look with my swollen eyes, no one's going to hire me. I don't look fresh. I look wiped out. You're not supposed to judge people by their looks, but people do."

'Black' Names Face Job Discrimination

While the West may pan India for its discrimination along caste lines in rural areas, discrimination of sorts is also practised in the US. A new study has found that when one is seeking a job in the land of freedom, the United States, it helps to have a white-sounding name.

Applications with white-sounding first names elicited 50 per cent more responses than ones with black-sounding names, says the study by professors at the University of Chicago Graduate School of Business and the Massachusetts Institute of Technology.

Responding to want ads in the *Boston Globe* and *Chicago Tribune*, the professors sent out some 5,000 resumes. The non-existent "white" applicants elicited one response (a call, letter or e-mail) for every 10 resumes mailed, while the "black" applicants with equal credentials received one response for every 15 resumes sent.

The study concluded that this difference was solely attributable to name manipulation. Said the study authors: "Our results so far suggest that there is a substantial amount of discrimination in the job recruiting process." The white names used included Neil, Brett, Greg, Emily, Anne and Jill. Some of the black names used were Tamika, Ebony, Aisha, Rasheed, Kareem and Tyrone.

Furthermore, companies that claimed to be equal opportunity employers were also no more likely to respond to black resumes than other businesses.

No wonder many Indians settled in the States have adopted English-sounding names – like Sam Pitroda or Dr Dicksheet!

Workers Want Flexi Hours, Not Higher Pay!

Workers the world over would do anything to get a higher pay packet, right? Wrong! According to a survey conducted by a UK recruitment consultancy and the government, workers would rather have flexible hours than extra pay, a company car or gym membership.

In the online poll, 46 per cent of the 4,000 respondents chose flexible hours as the perk they most wanted in a new job. A third of the new job seekers said they would rather have the chance to work flexi hours than to receive 1,000 pounds (approximately Rs.74,000) in extra pay.

The survey was conducted by the recruitment Website reed.co.uk and the Department of Trade and Industry and released on the eve of a government publicity campaign meant to increase awareness about new employment rights, beginning 6 April 2003.

The new rules have been described by the government as "family-friendly", which will allow workers with children under six or with disabled children under 18 to enjoy flexible working hours. According to government estimates, around 3.7 million worker-parents will be eligible to apply for the new working arrangements.